"It's clear that Greg really knows teens and has prayed with them. His ideas in *Teen Assemblies, Retreats and Prayer Services* are practical and very respectful of the reality of teenagers' lives and their search and struggle to grow spiritually. His choices of Scripture stories and the creative ways in which he uses them are excellent. The twenty prayer themes in this book are rich with imagery from Scripture, church tradition, and teenagers' own lives and concerns. I am eager to pray these services with the teens in my life."

Peg Bowman
Diocesan Director of Youth Ministry

"Greg Dues has created a marvelous resource here. In *Teen Assemblies, Retreats and Prayer Services*, young people are invited to be conscious of their own faith journey by entering into the faith journey of others. The themes are beautifully integrated with the seasons of the year. What a wonderful aid to those who work with youth, and what a wonderful gift to youth themselves."

Kevin Regan
Author, *Teen Prayer Services*

"Those who work with youth will find in these prayer experiences real opportunities to bring teenagers to an appreciation of prayer and Scripture in their own lives. No longer will youth ministers have to wrestle with the question, 'How can I help teenagers grow spiritually?' These prayer experiences genuinely help them to experience the presence of God in their lives. Dues uses Scripture themes to do this. His starting point is the Word of God concretely applied to their lives. He helps them 'wrestle with God,' and thus to experienrce the inspiration and healing power of Jesus."

Rev. J. Brian Beilman
Director of Religious Education
Archdiocese of Omaha

"In *Teen Assemblies, Retreats and Prayer Services* Greg Dues effectively links two vitally important components of sound adolescent evangelization and catechesis: an accessible use of Scripture and creative approaches to prayer. Each experience in the book helps young people prayerfully reflect on the personal and social implications of a particular biblical story or event. This approach reflects youth ministry at its best, and Greg has given all who work to pass on the gospel to young people a powerful tool for their ministry."

Tom Zanzig
Author, *Sharing* program and other books
for high schoolers
Presenter of youth ministry workshops

"If you're looking for a resource to engage older youth in Scripture reflection and prayer, *Teen Assemblies, Retreats and Prayer Services* will be a welcome addition to your youth ministry library. The themes are diverse and formats adaptable to a variety of settings. The reflections bring Scripture to life and make it relevant for youth who are searching for meaning in today's world."

Mary Lee Becker
Trainer, Consultant, Author in youth ministry
Bellevue, Washington

Searching for Faith

TEEN ASSEMBLIES
RETREATS and PRAYER SERVICES

GREG DUES

XXIII
TWENTY-THIRD PUBLICATIONS
Mystic, Connecticut 06355

Second printing 1995

Twenty-Third Publications
185 Willow Street
P.O. Box 180
Mystic CT 06355
(203) 536-2611
800-321-0411

ISBN 0-89622-561-5
Library of Congress Catalog Card Number 93-60027

To my co-ministers:

Rev. Dale Orlik
Kim Chenoweth

TABLE OF CONTENTS

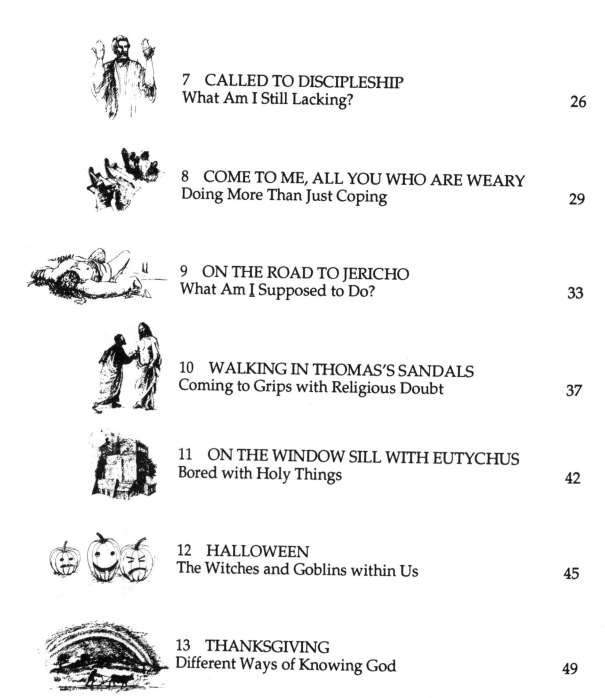

TEEN ASSEMBLIES
RETREATS and PRAYER SERVICES

INTRODUCTION

Most teenagers have completed eight or more years of religious formation. Many are still active in youth groups or in some kind of candidacy for confirmation. It's about this time that they arrive at a searching, disengaging, and even, for some, a *rejecting* stage of their faith. Religious faith, practice, and terminology they learned as children no longer guide many of them; more often than not, the subject bores them. Catholic traditions surrounding the sacraments, the unfolding of the church year, and parish life no longer excite them or even interest them as they did during childhood. Even God can become a bore—if there is a God as some are tempted to wonder!

Teen Assemblies, Retreats and Prayer Services invites teens to come to grips with feelings about religious matters and to pray about them. The themes unfold around a variety of prayer experiences and centering exercises that involve the teens in preparation, participation, activities, and discussion. Most of the themes and Scripture in this resource are seldom explored with young people. Therefore, there will be a freshness about them to engage the teens' imaginations, minds, and hearts.

Here is a brief overview of each of the twenty prayer-and-reflection sessions in this volume for the teens who are searching for faith:

1. Teenagers will meet a God who, as if in a game of hide and seek, enjoys hunting for them and being hunted by them in the searching phase of their teenage faith.

2. They find their own "Jacob's Ladder" (Genesis 28:10-19) when they experience breakthroughs to the mystery of God.

3. Along with this same patriarch, Jacob, they wrestle with God on the banks of their own River Jabbok (Genesis 32:23-33).

4. With Elijah, rejected and confused, the teens prayerfully hole up in the cave on Mt. Horeb, waiting for the God of tradition, but experiencing instead a God in a "tiny whispering sound" (1 Kings 19:1-13) passing through their very real life.

5. Moving on to the Christian Scriptures, the teens find a gentle healing power in Jesus.

6. Jesus, the teens will find, is their faithful companion.

7. Then they struggle with a Jesus who seems to expect too much from them (Matthew 19:16-22).

8. They find in Jesus the inspiration and power to cope with their adolescent problems and challenges.

9. They are challenged to find themselves in the parable of the Good Samaritan (Luke 10:25-37), in the beaten person, in those refusing to get involved, or in the Good Samaritan himself.

10. The teens are invited to walk in the sandals of doubting Thomas, struggling in prayer to believe what seems impossible, with only the testimony of others to go on (John 20:24-29).

11. They are invited to commiserate with the teenager who got so bored during the eucharist and with the apostle Paul's homily that he fell asleep and fell out of a third-story window (Acts 20:7-12)!

This same theme of searching faith is developed in several seasonal prayer assemblies:

12. The teens come to grips with the emotional and spiritual "witches and goblins" within them at Halloween time.

13. They celebrate different ways of talking about and knowing a gracious and bounteous God in the colors of fall and traditions of Thanksgiving.

14. At the beginning of Advent they celebrate a "Happy New Year" with a centering prayer leading them to appreciate their liturgical and popular traditions associated with solstices and equinoxes of the natural year.

15. They also prepare the way of the Lord during Advent with a reconcilation prayer service.

16-17. During Lent, they struggle with the crucial—*cross*—moments in their lives.

Several prayer assemblies are devoted to key religious symbols:

18. The teens sink their "old selves" in waters that become living waters.

19. They prayerfully become immersed in the symbols of Pentecost.

20. Finally, the teens come to reconciliation after dealing with their own temptations to run away from everything, as the Prodigal Son did (Luke 15:11-32), to follow their own directions, hunting for something that pleases them, regardless of their more fundamental relationships and responsibilities.

These themes are effective in teen retreats, catechetical situations, and various kinds of prayer services. In an adjusted form, they are also effective for adults (Note: A couple of these themes orginally appeared in a different form in my *Teaching Religion with Confidence and Joy*, Twenty-Third Publications, 1988).

There is no magic in any particular method, technique, or group dynamic in praying with teens. *Teen Assemblies, Retreats and Prayer Services* frequently uses a centering exercise or directed visualization as an option. These might also be called prayer fantasies. The teens are asked to relax and close their eyes. A leader directs them in the active use of the imagination regarding a particular theme. This focusing and quieting exercise with descriptive images encourages teens to center themselves, achieving a level of consciousness conducive to quiet prayer and communication with the Lord.

Other prayer forms are also used. There are suggestions for litanies, rituals of commitment, and prayers of thanksgiving and intercession.

A catechetical dimension supports all of these prayer assemblies in the form of introductions, preparation activities, and discussions. These prayer sessions also include reflection exercises to promote sharing and prayer. These, as with all suggestions in this resource, are intended only as samples and should be redesigned for your own needs. In fact, *these prayer assemblies have been written in such a way that some personal creative effort on the local level is called for and expected.* Teens need to be actively involved in their own group dynamics. Only with this involvement will their faith come alive and grow.

One dynamic used in most of these prayer sessions is a reflection, or sharing, sheet. The leader can design this to meet the needs of the group. These reflections, or group sharing, lead up to a closing prayer assembly.

There are references to a Prayer Table in some of these prayer assemblies. This contributes to the atmosphere of the assembly area and provides a focusing dynamic for the teens. A Prayer Table can be of any dimensions and covered with a brightly colored fabric. It should be large enough to hold a large colored, scented candle, along with other items, such as an open Bible, seasonal sacramentals, a basket for prayer cards that result from various prayer sessions. The Prayer Table becomes a sort of sanctuary that encourages sincere prayer. Use your own creativity and that of your teens.

Finally, the proclamation of Scripture is the energy source of most of these prayer assemblies. There is no single effective way, however, to proclaim this Scripture. Some youth leaders are more comfortable with a rather informal sharing of the Word; others prefer that it be proclaimed as written in a standard version of the Bible. Most readings in these prayer assemblies are cast in a narrative format, with several participants assigned parts to read.

I have used the *New Revised Standard Version, The New Oxford Annotated Bible* for readings, unless otherwise noted.

1
A HIDE
AND
SEEK GOD
A Searching Faith

Background Notes

Teens arrive at a *searching, disengaging,* and even, for some, a *rejecting* stage of their faith. This frustrates parents, teachers, and youth leaders even though they, too, experienced the same stage of faith years earlier. John W. Westerhoff III, in his *Will Our Children Have Faith?* observes: "In order to move from an understanding of faith that belongs to the community to an understanding of faith that is our own, we need to doubt and question that faith." This stage of faith is spiritually healthy. The wise adult is a patient, understanding, supportive, and gentle companion for teens during this time.

What seems at first to be spiritual rebellion among teens is often a form of disengagement instead. Other matters, such as the mysteries of puberty, confusion about relationships, demands of school work, part-time jobs, extra-curricular activities, and option shock about careers and future opportunities take priority over religious matters. Consequently, religious activities that seemed so important and even exciting to them as children now actually bore them. Feelings toward church and even toward God become all mixed up with feelings toward parents and other persons of authority.

Preparation

Discuss with the teens this natural searching stage of their faith. How does their current attitude toward religion compare with their attitude as children? How would they describe themselves: rebellious? disengaged? How do they understand these terms?

Prepare a reflection sheet with sharing questions and prayer assignment (see end of session). Card stock or large index cards will be practical if the teens are seated on the floor.

Assign the readings (Psalm 139, below). For greater variety and involvement from participants, the reading has been divided into several parts. Those chosen to read should have sufficient time to prepare. A prayer assembly, like parish liturgy, deserves sufficient preparation.

Finally, invite the teens to relax and to center their attention on the childhood game of "hide and seek" that they played so often. The ellipses (...) indicate a pause.

Invite them to recall their favorite hiding place ... How did they feel hiding? ... being hunted? ... How would they have felt if they had not been found? ... Ask them to imagine that God is hunting for them now ... Where are they hiding? ... In what preoccupations? ... In what sin?

Invite them to stay in this reflective mood of playing hide and seek with God as they listen to a reflective reading of Psalm 139.

Time to Listen
(Encourage a slow, reflective reading, with pauses between the sections.)

Reader 1:   O Lord, you have searched me and known me.
                    You know when I sit down and when I rise up;
                    you discern my thoughts from far away.
                    You search out my path and my lying down,
                    and are acquainted with all my ways.
                    Even before a word is on my tongue,
                    O Lord, you know it completely.

Reader 2:   You hem me in, behind and before,
                    and lay your hand upon me.
                    Such knowledge is too wonderful for me;
                    it is so high that I cannot attain it.
                    Where can I go from your spirit?
                    Or where can I flee from your presence?

Reader 3:   If I ascend to heaven, you are there;
                if I make my bed in Sheol, you are there.
                If I take the wings of the morning
                and settle at the farthest limits of the sea,
                even there your hand shall lead me,
                and your right hand shall hold me fast.

Reader 4:   If I say, "Surely the darkness shall cover me,
                and the light around me become night,"
                even the darkness is not dark to you;
                and the night is as bright as the day,
                and the darkness is as light to you.

Reader 5:   For it was you who formed my inward parts;
                you knit me together in my mother's womb.
                I praise you, for I am fearfully and wonderfully made.
                Wonderful are your works; that I know very well.
                My frame was not hidden from you,
                when I was being made in secret,
                intricately woven in the depths of Earth.

Reader 6:   Your eyes beheld my unformed substance.
                In your book were written all the days that
                were formed for me,
                when none of them as yet existed.
                How weighty to me are your thoughts, O God!
                How vast is the sum of them!
                I try to count them—they are more than the sand;
                I come to the end—I am still with you...

Response

Invite each teen to choose a partner. Ask them to stay in a prayerful, reflective mood as they share their thoughts and feelings. Hand out the reflection sheet. (Note: Design and make copies of a reflection sheet that will encourage sharing in your group. It might include what follows.)

REFLECTION SHEET

1. Have I ever felt like hiding from God? When? Why?
2. Where did I hide? (for example, distracting activities)
3. Did I ever feel that God had found me? What were the circumstances?

Complete the following as part of a prayer litany:
I hid from you, Lord, when

You found me, Lord, when

Assembly Prayer

Gather around a Prayer Table (see Introduction). Let the litany unfold, going from pair to pair. (Note: Some of these prayer "pieces" may be quite personal, and the teens reluctant to pray them aloud. It is always good to give teens the option of having the prayer sheets shuffled, returned, with all or some of the prayers being anonymous, or to have the leader pray them.)

Pray a final "collecting prayer" that reflects their pieces. Afterwards, gather the prayer sheets in a basket that stays on the Prayer Table. You might also end with a blessing. A great variety of blessings, including seasonal ones, are available in the parish Sacramentary.

2
JACOB'S LADDER
Celebrating Mystery in Life

Background Notes

Teens will readily relate to stories describing the ecstasies, agonies, and spiritual wanderings of biblical characters. These stories say a good deal about their own *searching stage* of faith. Teens, therefore, will gain further insight into their own searching by crawling inside a Bible story, feeling how the sandals of a woman or man of God fit *them!* Stories from our Hebrew Scriptures can have special effectiveness because they probably are new—and fresh—to the young people.

Teens, like all believers, need to interpret their experiences. Every moment of their lives and every cubic foot of their living space, playground, classroom, dance floor, and church can become a Jacob's ladder. This biblical image describes a breakthrough to the mystery dimension of all that is real in life. There are openings, so to speak, between us and God. These openings occur in our everyday living, working, praying, and playing. It is, then, in these breakthroughs, as Jacob experienced, that God "stands over" us, blessing us. Everything in our time and space becomes holy, a Jacob's ladder.

Preparation

Invite the teens to share some incidents in their lives when they felt a breakthrough to the mystery of God. (See the first prayer service.) Remind them that they need to interpret these experiences to find God. Faith gives them this ability to interpret.

Make sure the readings have been assigned and rehearsed.

In a previous session, or through your regular method of communication, invite the teens to bring to this assembly some personal symbolic "memorial stones" such as photos, precious memory things, or a souvenir. You might bring some of your own, too.

Prepare the Prayer Table as part of the assembly area for the response activity. Have the reflection sheets and pens available for the response activity.

Play centering music, encouraging the teens to enter the Bible story with their imaginations.

Time to Listen

Leader (setting the context of the story): The patriarch Jacob, son of Isaac, son of Abraham, stole his twin brother Esau's inheritance and God's special blessing that went along with it. He did this with the help from his mother, Rebecca. While Jacob is fleeing into exile to avoid being killed by Esau, God visits him in a dream. Jacob discovers that all space and time is sacred, full of the mystery of God.

Reader 1:

Jacob "came to a certain place and stayed there for the night, because the sun had set. Taking one of the stones of the place, he put it under his head and lay down in that place. And he dreamed that there was a ladder set up on the ground, the top of it reaching to the heaven; and the angels of God were ascending and descending on it. And the Lord stood beside him and said, '...know that I am with you and will keep you wherever you go, and will bring you back to this land; for I will not leave you until I have done what I have promised you.' Then Jacob woke from his sleep and said, 'Surely the Lord is in this place—and I did not know it!' And he was afraid, and said, 'How awesome is this place! This is none other than the house of God, and this is the gate of heaven'" (Genesis 28:11-17).

Reader 2:

"So Jacob rose early in the morning, and he took the stone that he had put under his head and set it up for a pillar and poured oil on the top of it. He called that place Bethel...saying, '...this stone, which I have set up for a pillar, shall be God's house...'" (Genesis 28:18-22).

Response

Remind the teens that memories, celebrations, and anniversaries are like Jacob's memorial stone. They mark those wonderful moments of breakthrough between us and God. Do the teens have any such "memorial stones"? Did they bring something to this assembly (see Preparation, above)? If so, invite them to place these on the Prayer Table in your assembly area. Special dates or anniversaries marked on a calendar are also examples of "Jacob's memorial stone."

Ask the teens to remain in a centered mood for a while. Give each a reflection sheet. While the centering music continues to play, the teens describe on the sheet a "Jacob's Ladder" experience in their own life, a time when they felt a breakthrough to God and God to them. They place these on the Prayer Table (which is symbolic of the "pillar" set up by Jacob).

(Note: Ask the teens to limit their reflection to positive and pleasant experiences. Another assembly will provide opportunity to discover mystery in painful experiences.)

REFLECTION SHEET

This is my personal "Jacob's Ladder" experience, a time when I felt a breakthrough between God and myself:

Assembly Prayer

When all are finished, they gather around the Prayer Table. The leader shuffles the reflection sheets and reads the testimonies. Invite the teens to respond with a prayer invocation such as: "For this memory, we praise you, Lord...." In all activities like this, give the teens the freedom to read their own personal testimony.

Invite the teens to bring more "memorial stones" to the Prayer Table in future assemblies. Gradually it will become a "pillar" marking the place of "God's house."

End with the blessing God gave to Jacob:

"Know that I am with you
and will keep you wherever you go...
I will not leave you
until I have done what I have promised you."

(You might bless each teen, with a laying on of hands.)

3

ON THE BANKS
OF THE RIVER
JABBOK
Wrestling With God

Background Notes

Teens naturally feel a certain amount of spiritual confusion as they make the transition from the learned religion of childhood to the searching faith of adolescence. Where is God? Who is God? At one time God seemed so evident, so important in life, but now there seems to be so much emptiness, a kind of personal spiritual vacuum. A willingness to struggle with these questions—in fact, to struggle with God in a very deliberate way—can lead to deeper faith and exciting insights: in the darkness of my spiritual struggle, God is closer to me than at any other time. It is at such times that I could almost name this God.

This experience of wrestling with the mystery of God becomes concrete in the dark moments of emotional pain, loss, and fear. Adults do not have a corner on such experiences. Teens may experience loss in an even more excruciating way because their lives are still fresh and new; time and repetition have not yet anaesthetized them to suffering. Their experiences often leave them wounded emotionally, physically, and spiritually.

Preparation

Have the readings below rehearsed by teens. Prepare the reflection sheet as well as a poster with the final prayer response (see below).

Light a candle on the Prayer Table and set the mood for this prayerful centering exercise by sharing thoughts from Background Notes above. Draw out from the teens some areas of spiritual struggles that they or peers have experienced. Some doubts of faith? Some instances of anger with God, or feeling abandoned by God? You might put these topics on the board or on paper taped to the wall. Adult leaders or guests, invited to this session, might "prime the pump" by sharing some of their own faith struggles.

Invite the teens to center themselves. Play calming background music.

Time to Listen

Leader (setting the context): Jacob spent most of his adult life in exile, blessed by God with a large family and wealth, but far away from his brother. One day he decides to return to the land of his birth and to be reconciled with the twin brother he had cheated so many years before. The night before he arrived in his brother's territory, he went off alone to the banks of the River Jabbok. There he wrestled all night with God, thinking at first that it was an ordinary man.

Narrator: Jacob was left alone; and a man wrestled with him until daybreak. When the man saw that he did not prevail against Jacob, he struck him on the hip socket; and Jacob's hip was put out of joint as he wrestled with him. Then the man said:

God: Let me go, for the day is breaking.

Jacob: I will not let you go, unless you bless me.

God: What is your name?

Jacob: Jacob.

God: You shall no longer be called Jacob, but Israel, for you have striven with God and with humans, and have prevailed.

Jacob: Please tell me your name.

God: Why do you ask my name?

Narrator: And there he blessed him. So Jacob called the place Peniel, saying,

Jacob: I have seen God face to face, and yet my life is preserved (Genesis 32:24-32).

Response

Continue the centering exercise, using the reflection sheet below. Invite the teens to recall a time when they were full of doubts about the existence of God, full of doubts about the power and love of God. With their eyes closed, invite them to sink into the darkness of these experiences. Invite them to wrestle now in spirit with the all-powerful God—on the banks of their own River Jabbok.

After a while, ask the teens to record their insights.

REFLECTION SHEET

I felt I was struggling with God when

I felt a personal "wounding" that reminded me of my own weakness and God's loving power when

Assembly Prayer

Let the teens gather around the Prayer Table. Collect and shuffle the reflection sheets and place them on the altar. Conclude the assembly with prayers similar to the following formulas:

All: I wrestled with you, Lord, when
   (Invite individual teens to insert a brief experience here from their reflection sheet, or read one from an anonymous sheet on the Prayer Table. You might conclude each with a prayer response like the following.)

All: I have seen God face to face—and have been blessed.
   (Continue this prayer period as long as feasible.)

4
IN THE
CAVE ON
MOUNT HOREB
Hearing God's Whisper

Background Notes

Teens sometimes feel as though they don't know who God is any more. When they were younger, it all seemed to fit together better. Traditional images of God, while not exactly understood, were accepted as the real thing. They found God in church decorations, stained-glass windows, pictures in their religion books, in popular prayer formulas, in religious vocabulary, sacraments, and symbols. Now, during their searching stage of faith, their ability to recognize God, to sense God's presence, seems to be falling all apart. Religious images from their childhood do not seem to fit their personal needs and convictions now.

Humans have always been searching creatures. From the big question marks of unrecorded history to the hundreds of separate religions today, the search for God goes on. It is because people *search* that the wonder of finding mystery once in a while is all the more enjoyable. This search happens for most people within an organized community of believers, under the guidance of religious leaders. For teens it happens in religious education sessions, youth group meetings, during homilies at Mass, during retreats. At times, however, the search must be a private struggle in the aloneness of one's own faith.

There is a surprise waiting for teens who are willing to search for the mystery of God: the God whom they discover is not always the God they are looking for. The God of teen years differs from the one they experienced as children. And different from the one they will enjoy at other times in life.

Preparation

Some time in advance, invite the teens to use their creativity to saturate the assembly area with traditional images of God. Use art paper, poster paper, and collages of pictures from magazines. Borrow religious art from the nooks and crannies of the parish buildings and homes of parishioners. If there is time, create bold murals with tempera paint. If pictures are not available, substitute descriptive words. Assign the readings below and have the reflection question and a card for a litany ready.

Time to Listen

Leader (setting the context): Almost a thousand years after the patriarch Jacob discovered his God on the banks of the River Jabbok (see previous prayer session), God sent his prophet Elijah to scold the descendants of Jacob for drifting away from the true God. In doing so, Elijah incurred the wrath of the wicked queen Jezebel. He had to escape into exile to avoid execution. After 40 days and nights traveling through the desert, he hid in a cave on Mt. Horeb, the "mountain of God." There for a fleeting moment Elijah experienced a God very different from the one he was used to in his religious traditions.

Reader 1: "The word of the LORD came to him, saying, 'Go out and stand on the mountain before the LORD; the LORD will be passing by.' A strong and heavy wind was rending the mountains and crushing rocks before the LORD—but the LORD was not in the wind.

Reader 2: After the wind there was an earthquake, but the LORD was not in the earthquake. After the earthquake there was fire, but the LORD was not in the fire.

Reader 3: After the fire there was a tiny whispering sound. When he heard this, Elijah hid his face in his cloak and went and stood at the entrance of the cave" (1 Kings 19:11-13, New American Bible).

Leader: Up until this moment in the cave, Elijah had known God only in traditional terms: a nomadic God of shepherds and desert sheiks, a mystery God who spoke to Moses out of a burning bush, a liberating God of Moses who led the people to freedom from slavery in Egypt, a God who inflicted enemies of

Israel with horrible plagues, a God who guided them through the desert wilderness with a pillar of fire and cloud of smoke, a God of awesome appearances amid fire and smoke on holy mountains, a warrior God who led them to victory over enemies in battle after battle, a God who seemed pleased with burning sacrifices offered on the temple altar, a scolding God who spoke through prophets, a tender and loving God who was always willing to forgive....

Now, just for a moment, Elijah experiences a different God: a quiet, peaceful God just passing by! This God who appears as "a tiny whisper just passing by" has important implications for anyone searching for God. A tiny whisper is a very delicate communication. It calls for a delicate environment or it will not be heard. God seldom comes in an Earth-shattering way.

Response

Invite the teens to rest for a while with this God who comes in a "tiny whispering sound." Have them recall a moment or situation in their own lives when they experienced God in this quiet, simple way; for example, in a gentle hug, in sunrises and sunsets, in quiet moments, or in a kind word.

Invite them to pick a prayer partner and share their experiences. As this sharing tapers off, ask each pair to prepare a litany card, something like the following form.

REFLECTION SHEET

Lord, I found you whispering when:

Assembly Prayer

With the teens gathered around the Prayer Table and with candle lit, share these prayerful experiences reflectively in a litany style. Afterwards, ask for volunteers to print these prayer testimonies with colorful marking pens to add to the room atmosphere for future prayer assemblies.

5
ARE YOU THE ONE?
Identifying Our Savior

Background Notes

Jesus is the best example of how delicately and softly God comes among us (see Prayer Session 4). God did not come to live with us in some Earth-shaking way. God's whisper, God's Word, was made flesh and began life in the quiet poverty of a cave stable in Bethlehem. Outside of his own extended family and insignificant hometown of Nazareth, Jesus was not heard of until his River Jordan "coming out" as a mature man. After that, he was popular with many people, but his influence was delicate. He used a quiet approach in teaching a new gospel. He told challenging parables and stories. His contact with people, too, was just as delicate: chatting with the woman at the well, patiently explaining new ideas to Nicodemus, quietly protecting the woman taken in adultery, kicking off his sandals and visiting with his friends Mary and Martha and Lazarus.

Preparation

Invite the teens to share their current impressions of who Jesus was. Record these on posterboard or wall charts. How would they describe him? What mental images do they have of him? If Jesus had lived in our own time, where would we find him? How would he look? What causes would he champion?

Traditional images might be exhibited in the assembly area ahead of time. Some contemporary images might also be exhibited, for example, the popular "laughing Jesus" ("Jesus Christ Liberator" by W. Wheatley, 1973).

Do an imagination exercise after the fashion of *Back to the Future* (Part 1). If they could travel back to Galilee and spend a week with Jesus, what do they think they would? experience? Then ask them to hold on to these thoughts and feelings as they listen to Scripture. Have the readings assigned and rehearsed and the prayer card ready for a testimony response later.

Time to Listen

Leader (setting the context): Jesus had a quiet, healing touch. His was not the pretentious, "show biz" healing sessions we know from the old revival meetings and some TV preachers. Rather, his was an effective, gentle response to what was needed at the moment. His healing ministry was joined to a teaching ministry. His message gave people a purpose to live for; it gave their lives meaning. John the Baptist, in prison for his own preaching, heard about his cousin Jesus and wondered what was happening.

Narrator: The disciples of John reported to him what Jesus was teaching and doing. So John summoned two of his disciples and sent them to Jesus to ask, "Are you the one who is to come, or are we to wait for another? When the men came to Jesus they said,

John's Disciples: John the Baptist has sent us to ask whether you are the one we have been expecting, or should watch for someone else?

Narrator: Jesus had just then cured many people of diseases and freed them from evil spirits; he had given sight to many who were blind. So he answered them,

Jesus: Go and tell John what you have seen and heard: the blind receive their sight, the lame walk, the lepers are cleansed, the deaf hear, the dead are raised, the poor have the good news brought to them. And blessed is anyone who takes no offense at me (Luke 7:18-23).

Response

Create a centering atmosphere of silence, or silence with background music. Challenge the teens to identify Jesus' healing touch and healing word in their own lives. This healing may have touched some emotional or psychological problem, some fear or bothersome attitude, or an illness. Remind them that the healing presence of Jesus is usually not spectacular, but very gentle and quiet. It may touch them through a friend, parent, doctor, counselor, teacher, priest, Scripture.

REFLECTION SHEET

As in previous assemblies, it might be helpful for the teens to share with a prayer partner. Sometimes, however, teens prefer that their reflection remain private. After they have identified a healing touch of Jesus or a need for his healing touch, ask them to summarize their experiences by writing it down on a prayer card, such as the following:

Jesus' healing power touched me when:

(Or) Thank you, Lord, for touching me with your healing power when:

Assembly Prayer

End this prayer session with a period of testimony as the teens share their experiences. Or, with the teens gathered around the Prayer Table, the testimony cards are shuffled, with anonymous prayers offered by a leader, or by the teens if they wish to offer their own. Finally, conclude with a spontaneous thanksgiving or petition prayers for healing.

6

AT HOME WITH JESUS
God as My Companion

Background Notes

There is nothing more precious than a true friend. If that friend is also a *companion*, then we enjoy something even more wonderful. The word "companion" originated in Latin (*pan*, bread; *cum*, with) and meant a person "with whom we break bread." Today we might say "a person with whom we share a Coke and fries." Or, a person we feel at home with. A companion, therefore, is someone we trust completely, with whom we can share our most secret thoughts and hopes, who travels through life with us, someone we want by our side in the best of times and in the worst of times. If we have such a companion, we are never lonely. Experiencing Jesus as a true friend and companion is essential to Christian faith. It is a key element in the religious life of teens.

Preparation

Have Bibles available. Prepare the "Jesus Is a Companion" sheet. Prepare the assembly area for a centering exercise or prayer fantasy. Some effective techniques for centering are soothing background music, subdued lighting, a special location: for example, a carpeted chapel floor.

Time to Listen

(Note: This centering exercise should be adapted by the one leading it. Its pace should be very slow—almost hypnotic.)

Leader: Imagine someone you can be completely at ease with ... a very special friend ... a person you can share your most secret thoughts with ... your problems ... plans ... hopes ... Invite that person to go for a walk with you ... Walk to a favorite place where you can be comfortable and alone with your companion ... and can talk with each other without interruption ... (long pause) ... Now that you are there, talk with your friend about the most important thing in your life ... It may be something very happy and exciting ... It may be something sad ... or something you're hoping for ... Talk with your companion about whatever is most important to you at this moment ... Your companion listens as no one has ever listened to you before ... (long pause) ... Now your companion talks to you ... what is your companion saying? ... How does it make you feel? ... (after sufficient reflection) ... Now begin to come back to the present ... to this place ... Bring your feelings with you ... (Long pause to allow the teens to regroup in spirit and body).

Leader (after the teens have regrouped): Companionship is a fundamental need in human life. The earliest followers of Jesus enjoyed a companionship with him. Some may have known him as a childhood friend; some were related to him by blood. Some discovered him as a companion during his travels around the country as a religious teacher. Some, like the apostles, lived with him; others found him in a particular moment of need. As he walked along the dusty roads of Palestine, Jesus was a companion to people: at meals and parties, camping out at night, teaching on the hillsides, taking care of the sick and the rejected. Jesus tended to spend time at table with people who had been rejected by others. He stayed close to people and they knew him as human like themselves. They were never alone; he seemed to

be everything they needed. Once he became their companion, their life changed; it took on new meaning. Only later would they know why.

Response

Invite the teens to share what they felt during the centering exercise. How many feelings from their human companionship with peers can they associate with their companionship with Jesus? Encourage, but do not force, some honest testimony. Divide the teens into groups of four. Give each teen a Bible and a reflection sheet. Assign one or two of the gospel stories listed below to each group. Ask them to read the Scripture stories privately and to share their insights that the Scripture reveals to them. Encourage them to get inside the feelings of the characters in the story. They may use the questions below to help them reflect on the stories.

1. Jesus calls Levi (Mark 2:13-17)
2. The Transfiguration (Mark 9:2-9)
3. Jesus blesses little children (Mark 10:13-16)
4. Jesus prays in Gethsemane (Mark 14:32-40)
5. Jesus visits Martha and Mary (Luke 10:38-42)
6. Jesus and Nicodemus (John 3:1-21)
7. Jesus and the Samaritan woman (John 4:5-30)
8. Jesus weeps (John 11:28-37)
9. Jesus is anointed at Bethany (Matthew 26:6-13)

REFLECTION SHEET

1. What companionship qualities of Jesus do you find in this Scripture story?

2. What have you experienced in your own life that is similar to what you see in this story?

3. How would you feel if you were in this story?

4. Who do you know that possesses some of these qualities of Jesus?

My Prayer

At the conclusion of the shared reflection, ask each teen to compose a brief prayer on their sheet, using the theme and spirit of the assigned Scripture stories.

Assembly Prayer

Let the teens gather around the Prayer Table. Invite them to pray what they have written. Encourage them to take the prayer with them and pray it frequently before the next session.

Other Options

There are other ways to let this prayer session unfold. For example, after their own reflection, each group might join another to share their stories and discoveries. If the teens enjoyed a certain story, make sure they can locate it in the Bible for future reflection. You might also challenge the teens to design their own fantasy centering prayer from one or more of the Scripture stories above, making it fit their contemporary teen life. This might be used in a future prayer session. Or, challenge small groups of teens to role-play one of the assigned stories as a mime, challenging other teens to guess the story. Can they make it fit their contemporary teen scene?

7
CALLED
TO
DISCIPLESHIP
What Am I Still Lacking?

Background Notes

Jesus calls each of us to discipleship: "Come, follow me!" This call to follow Jesus has practical ramifications for teens faced with crucial decisions about such things as relationships, work, college, career choices, sexuality, cultural values, philosophy of life, recreation, clothes, and acquisition and the use of money. Jesus did not design a single category into which all his followers had to fit. Nor does he expect the same thing from each person today. Rather, his call is very personal, tailor-made to each person, so to speak. The only way to discover one's own call to discipleship is to develop an openness to the presence of Jesus, listening carefully to what he asks of me—here and now. His call will often come through some ordinary means—possibly this prayer session.

Preparation

Ask the teens to draw pictures of or to print in bold letters words that describe their favorite possessions. Use watercolor marking pens, construction paper, art paper, plain paper, large sheets of butcher paper, etc. The words should reflect all the usual concerns of teens' life: clothes, money, leisure time, bicycles, cars, jewelry, pets, friends, swimming pools, TVs, radios, etc. Prepare the atmosphere of the assembly area by having the teens hang these sheets of paper all over. Assign the Scripture reading and prepare the Discipleship Card. Print a large poster with the teens' commitment prayer (see Response, below).

Time to Listen

Leader (setting the context): Jesus was not a harsh teacher. He did not demand the impossible of his followers, nor ask the same thing of everyone. He was not satisfied that his followers be faithful only to the traditional morality of the times. He expected a great deal from his followers, and wasn't afraid to say so.

Narrator: As Jesus was setting out on a journey, a man ran up and knelt before him, and asked:

Questioner: Good Teacher, what must I do to inherit eternal life?

Narrator: Jesus said to him,

Jesus: Why do you call me good? No one is good but God alone. You know the commandments: "You shall not murder; you shall not commit adultery; you shall not steal; you shall not bear false witness; you shall not defraud; honor your father and mother."

Questioner: Teacher, I have kept all these commandments since my youth.

Narrator: Jesus, looking at him, loved him and said,

Jesus: You lack one thing: go, sell what you own, and give the money to the poor, and you will have treasure in heaven. Then come, follow me.

Narrator: When the man heard this, he was shocked and went away grieving, for he had many possessions (Mark 10:17-22).

Response

First, invite the teens to respond to this reading from the heart. What emotions do they feel? Frustration? Anger? Defensive of the man in the gospel story? Having heard the teens' responses, what words describing their own personal preoccupations and possessions stand out? What might Jesus be asking of them?

REFLECTION SHEET

Ask each teen to reflect on these important questions for a while. Then ask each to fill out a Discipleship Card, responding to this challenge:

"The following is one thing still lacking in me that I feel Jesus is asking. I am willing to try to do this one thing more!"

Assembly Prayer

After the cards are filled out, invite the teens to present them—but not to read them—at the Prayer Table, preferably one by one, using a formula like this (printed on a poster): Lord, you ask a lot of me, but never too much. Accept this small pledge of my discipleship. Amen.

8
COME TO ME, ALL YOU WHO ARE WEARY
Doing More Than Just Coping

Background Notes

Viktor Frankl, a Jewish psychiatrist who survived a concentration camp during the Holocaust, emphasizes that we live only as long we have a meaning to live for. Each year thousands of teens decide to stop living and take their lives in suicide. It is unknown how many more try to die. Some of these seem to have despaired in situations similar to those commonly experienced by their peers. Their feelings were so terribly low that the meaning of life just slipped away—if it was ever there.

Adolescence is a time of many crises: from zits to broken hearts. Every human life is full of crises as the years go by. We learn to cope with them simply by going through them repeatedly. We do more than cope; we grow and mature through these experiences. Sometimes we feel a sense of victory and march on. At other times we fail miserably, go into a funk for weeks, and just can't seem to get started again. Any meaning to live for starts to fade.

Preparation

Have Bibles available. Prepare a "Jesus Helps Me Cope" reflection sheet. Prepare the assembly area in such a way that a prayerful centering exercise or prayer fantasy can take place effectively (see Prayer Session 7).

Time to Listen

(Note: This centering exercise should be adapted by the one leading it. Its pace should be very slow—almost hypnotic—with pauses.)

Leader: Imagine a time when you felt as lousy as a person can feel ... when you were down as low as you can get ... when there seemed to be no place to run to ... no one to turn to ... Maybe you're going through something right now ... Get in touch with that no-good feeling ... the feeling of failure ... the feeling of loneliness ... the feeling of conflict ... the feeling of being rejected ... betrayed ... the feeling of being a misfit ... the feeling of being in sin ... Maybe there is no one to talk to ... or those who listen just brush aside what is bothering you ... Family problems are getting worse each day ... It's impossible to get a job ... Things can seem so black ... so empty ... so worthless ... Sometimes it seems there's just no meaning left in life ... Get in touch with your lowest moment ... your lowest feeling ... (long pause).

Who was there supporting you in that low moment? ... Think about that person ... (long pause).

Now listen to these words of Scripture that Jesus speaks to you now: "Come to me, all you that are weary and are carrying heavy burdens, and I will give you rest ... Come to me, all you that are weary and are carrying heavy burdens, and I will give you rest" (Matthew 11:28) ... Sometimes Jesus helps us cope ... and to do more than just cope ... to actually grow and mature through a crisis ... He does this by his wonderful and powerful love ... Sometimes he does this through the hands and words of others.

(after sufficient reflection) Now begin to come back to the present ... to this place ... knowing that there is someone always with you to help you cope with any crisis or problem ... and to grow through the crisis ... (Long pause to allow the teens to regroup in spirit and body).

Leader (after the teens have come back to the present): We have a choice when we are down low. We can choose to stay down in despair: letting go of any meaning to live for. Or we can choose to reach out to someone else, grabbing hold of their strength, love, power, and answers. The one who has all this, all the time, and who is always with us, is Jesus Christ. It is the experience of many believers that they find Jesus at the moment when they have no other person to turn to. In that moment they reach out and find a God who gives them a reason to live and a Jesus he sent to be with us. Often this presence of Jesus actually comes through the presence and help offered by friends, family, and teachers, or even by strangers.

Scripture does not have an index called "Problems and How to Cope with Them." It is not the purpose of Scripture to give quick and easy answers. Rather, it gives meanings to live for. And it puts us in contact with a Christ who is always with us with a powerful love and meaningful answer. When we reach out to this Christ, we will find our crises and problems touched with this powerful love—and meaningful answers.

Response

Invite the teens to share what they felt during the centering exercise. How many of these feelings are shared by their peers, by those present? Encourage, but do not force, some honest testimony. Divide the group into small groups. Give each teen a Bible and a reflection sheet with key Scripture readings and discussion topics (see below). Mark one or more key gospel stories for each group. Ask them to read the Scripture privately. Then reflect with them on the truth that Jesus is always present, helping us cope. How do his words play out in their life? "Come to me, all you that are weary and are carrying heavy burdens, and I will give you rest." Encourage them to get inside the feelings of the characters in the story. Challenge them to fit their own life experiences into the story.

Ask them to share how Jesus has helped them through others. Their reflection sheet will provide key questions. After a sufficient time for reflecting on this, ask each teen to compose a brief prayer on their sheet, using the theme and spirit of the assigned Scripture.

REFLECTION SHEET

(Note: Most of the gospel stories on the reflection sheet concern physical healing or driving out evil. Explain to the teens that these stories speak clearly of a Jesus who has power over all kinds of evil, including physical, emotional, mental, and spiritual.)

1. Jesus heals a person with skin disease (Luke 5:12-16)
2. Jesus heals a paralyzed person (Luke 5:17-26)
3. Jesus heals a foreigner's servant (Luke 7:1-10)
4. Jesus brings to life a widow's son (Luke 7:11-17)
5. Jesus heals a person with demons (Luke 8:26-39)
6. Jesus heals a woman (Luke 8:40-48)
7. Jesus heals a boy with a demon (Luke 9:37-43)
8. Jesus heals a crippled woman (Luke 13:10-17)

9. Jesus heals a crippled person (Luke 14:1-6)

10. Jesus heals ten men who have a skin disease (Luke 17:11-19)

Reflection Questions

1. What is the person coping with in the story? What is the crisis? What crisis in teen life today, similar to it, could be substituted in that story?

2. What words in Scripture describe a "reaching out" to Jesus? What words would you use in a contemporary situation?

3. What does Jesus ask of the person in crisis? Of the bystanders?

4. Have you ever reached out to Jesus with faith in a time of crisis? If so, describe the situation briefly. Was Jesus there when you reached out? Explain your feelings.

Personal Prayer

Invite the teens to write a personal prayer based on the reflection just concluded.

Assembly Prayer

Gather around the Prayer Table. Invite the teens to pray the prayer they wrote. Encourage them to take their prayer with them and pray it frequently before the next session.

9

ON THE ROAD TO JERICHO
What Am I Supposed to Do?

Background Notes

Jesus had a knack of turning current moral convictions upside down and inside out! His parables reflect this pattern. They express the unexpected. What he really wants is a behavior that is quite different from our usual behavior.

This is clearly seen in Jesus' parable of the Good Samaritan (Luke 10:25-37). No one in this parable acts the way people would expect. The priest and Levite would have been expected to help a fellow Jew because, after all, they represented the highest religious leadership and it was their religious duty to be compassionate and help the wounded man. A Samaritan, on the other hand, would not have been expected to show any sympathy to a Jew because of the history of hatred between Jews and Samaritans. But the unexpected happens in the parable. Jesus' message packs a real moral punch.

Teens, like all followers of Jesus, are challenged to live this parable in their own day-to-day world. But peer pressure and pressure from the prevalent attitudes in society often influence them to act in a way contrary to gospel morality. They often run into situations where someone needs help or attention of some kind, but they are tempted to walk by, close their eyes, and avoid getting involved. But Jesus says: "Stop, love, care, respond...."

Preparation

Make sure the gospel reading has been rehearsed. This prayer session leads up to a commitment ritual. Prepare the reflection sheet and commitment poster (see Response, below).

Time to Listen

Leader (setting the context): The stories that Jesus told often have a surprise ending. They challenge our usual way of understanding and doing things. One day a lawyer wanted to test Jesus. Listen to the parable Jesus told.

Lawyer: Teacher, what must I do to inherit eternal life?

Jesus: You shall love the Lord your God with all your heart, and with all your soul, and with all your strength, and with all your mind; and your neighbor as yourself.

Lawyer: And who is my neighbor?

Jesus: A man was going down from Jerusalem to Jericho, and fell into the hands of robbers, who stripped him, beat him, and went away, leaving him half dead. Now by chance a priest was going down that road; and when he saw him, he passed by on the other side. So likewise a Levite, when he came to the place and saw him, passed by on the other side. But a Samaritan while traveling came near him; and when he saw him, he was moved to pity. He went to him and bandaged his wounds, having poured oil and wine on them. Then he put him on his own animal, brought him to an inn, and took care of him. The next day he took out two denarii, gave them to the innkeeper, and said, "Take care of him; and when I come back, I will repay you whatever more you spend." *Which of these three, do you think, was a neighbor to the man who fell into the hands of the robbers?*

Lawyer: The one who showed him mercy.

Jesus: Go and do likewise.

Response

Challenge the teens to apply this parable to a contemporary situation. Divide the them into smaller groups of 5 or 6. Using a reflection sheet, assign one area of real life to each group: school, neighborhood, parish, business world (their own jobs, the mall). Each group is asked to discuss some real situation that is similar to the one in this parable of the Good Samaritan. Remind them that the situation need not be about a physical mugging and beating. It may deal with the emotions, some kind of rejection, or with some form of dishonesty, prejudice, civil rights, etc. Who is hurting and in need of assistance or comfort? Who is avoiding the obligation to be helpful? Who is offering help? What would Jesus expect of each of the situations they are discussing?

Then have each group prepare one "Good Samaritan" scenario or role-play in which there is hurt, rejection, avoidance, and care.

REFLECTION SHEET

With your group design a "Good Samaritan" story that takes place in one of the following settings:

- School
- Neighborhood
- Parish
- Business world

Reflection Questions

Identify a real situation from your own experience, or from what you have heard or seen on TV or in a movie.

1. In this real situation,

Who is hurting?

Who is avoiding help? How?

Who is helping or could help? How?

What would the Jesus-answer be?

2. What *could* you do in this situation? What *would* you do?

3. Plan a role-play of this scenario.

Finally, invite each group to role-play their scene and testify to a behavior that they hear Jesus asking of them.

Assembly Prayer

Lead the teens in a commitment ritual. Ahead of time, print on a poster the commitment formula: "When I know of someone who is hurting, I will stop and care!" After the role-plays, gather the teens around the Prayer Table. Proclaim the hurt that was emphasized in each role-play. The teens reply with the commitment formula. For example: *Classmates are made fun of because of the way they dress:* "*When I know of someone who is hurting, I will stop and care!*"

Challenge the teens to be extra sensitive during the coming week to situations that involve some kind of hurt. Ask them to take daily inventory of their *spontaneous* feelings. How do these feelings reflect those of a "Good Samaritan"?

10
WALKING IN THOMAS'S SANDALS
Coming to Grips with Religious Doubt

Background Notes

The gospel story of "doubting Thomas" (John 20:19-29) reflects the attitude of many teens. They spent numerous years faithfully "learning their religion" and preparing to receive the sacraments. Now traditional faith isn't as exciting as preparing for First Communion or other significant events in earlier years. They are not making some clear-cut decision against the mystery of Jesus or church. Rather, matters of faith do not always fare well in competition with the raging battles of adolescent hormones, relationship problems, peer pressures, the shock of choosing among dozens of options regarding careers, and fallout from the generation gap.

What is happening is natural and normal. These teens have arrived at another stage of faith—not a denial of faith. They are questioning, searching, challenging, and even disengaging themselves from organized religion. Catechists, youth ministers, and priests continue to testify to the wonders of Christian mysteries: "We have seen the Lord!" But now, speaking from the midst of normal distractions, compounded by challenging attitudes toward authority and despair in the face of overwhelming expectations, teens tend to ignore and to reject the testimony of authority figures. In so many words, they say: "Show me. I don't believe what you are saying."

Preparation

Have the gospel reading rehearsed. Prepare the reflection sheet and activity that leads up to the concluding prayer.

Time to Listen

Leader (setting the context): When Jesus was arrested, most of his friends and disciples fled in panic and despair. Three days later, hiding out in the Upper Room, they were faced with the unexpected.

Narrator: When it was evening on that day, the first day of the week, and the doors of the house where the disciples had met were locked for fear of the Jews, Jesus came and stood among them and said:

Jesus: Peace be with you.

Narrator: After he said this, he showed them his hands and his side. Then the disciples rejoiced when they saw the Lord. Jesus said to them again:

Jesus: Peace be with you. As the Father has sent me, so I send you.

Narrator: When he had said this, he breathed on them and said to them:

Jesus: Receive the Holy Spirit. If you forgive the sins of any, they are forgiven them; if you retain the sins of any, they are retained.

Narrator: But Thomas (who was called the Twin), one of the twelve, was not with them when Jesus came. So the other disciples told him,

Disciples: We have seen the Lord.

Thomas: Unless I see the mark of the nails in his hands, and put my finger in the mark of the nails and my hand in his side, I will not believe.

Narrator: A week later his disciples were again in the house, and Thomas was with them. Although the doors were shut, Jesus came and stood among them and said,

Jesus: Peace be with you.

Narrator: Then he said to Thomas:

Jesus: Put your finger here and see my hands. Reach out your hand and put it in my side. Do not doubt but believe.

Narrator: Thomas answered him,

Thomas: My Lord and my God!

Narrator: Jesus said to him:

Jesus: Have you believed because you have seen me? Blessed are those who have not seen and yet have come to believe.

Response

Using the reflection sheet, challenge the teens to find themselves in this gospel story. Before that, invite each one to reflect silently:

1. on something in traditional Catholicism/Christianity that they do not believe at present

2. on something that supports their faith in Jesus.

(Note: This reflection topic deals with what teens accept as evidence for their personal faith: symbolically the "wounds" in the hands and side of Jesus that they have seen, so to speak.)

REFLECTION SHEET

I'm a Doubting Thomas, too! (This is something I don't believe at present, or at least have a more difficult time believing than I did before.)

This Is Something That Supports My Faith:

Assembly Prayer

After the teens have identified their own "doubting Thomas" area of their faith, invite them to participate in the following ritual. (Note: Make sure the teens understand that it is all right to struggle with faith, to doubt, to challenge their religious traditions.)

All Teens: We have seen the Lord!

"Doubting Thomas": (A volunteer teen stands and insists on her (his) own lack of belief [from the Reflection Sheet, above]. Then the rest are encouraged to testify to their own faith in regard to the lack of faith just expressed, trying to persuade their peer "doubting Thomas." Then the ritual continues.)

All Teens: We have seen the Lord!

"Doubting Thomas": (Another volunteer teen stands and insists on her (his) own lack of belief [from the Reflection Sheet, above]. This process continues until the end of the session.

Invite the teens to place their reflection sheets on the Prayer Table.

Praying with Our Bodies

This would be a good opportunity to lead the teens in prayer with their bodies, using one or more traditional ritual positions: prostration, genuflection, bowing. While the entire group solemnly proclaims the words of Thomas, "My Lord and my God," invite them to prostrate briefly ... or to genuflect slowly ... or to bow deeply. Try to have the group do this very deliberately—ritually—even using liturgical "dance."

You might share the following information with the teens:

Prostration: An intense, total, and dramatic expression of adoration, penance, or supplication. It was common among ancient peoples and from them passed into Christian tradition. Jesus himself prayed this way in the Garden of Gethsemane the night before he died: "He advanced a little and fell prostrate in prayer" (Matthew 26:39). A full prostration by the priests began each Mass until after the early Middle Ages. It is still retained at the beginning of the Good Friday liturgy.

Genuflection: A gesture peculiar to Catholics is that of genuflecting before entering a church pew. This is a sign of adoration and greeting directed toward the divine presence of the Blessed Sacrament reserved in the tabernacle in the sanctuary. Today it is common that the Blessed Sacrament and the tabernacle be located in a special chapel separated from the sanctuary. Many parishioners still genuflect out of habit, even though the Blessed Sacrament is not present.

Bowing: The gesture of bowing has always been the custom of Catholics in the Eastern church, instead of genuflecting. In the Western church it was a popular tradition to bow slightly when the name of Jesus and even Mary occurred in prayer. A more profound bow always substitutes for a genuflection.

Both the genuflection (Latin, "bending of the knee") and the bow are symbolic of one's smallness, or humility, in the presence of the greatness of the Lord. These devotional gestures were borrowed from court etiquette of the Roman Empire, which in turn had borrowed them from oriental courts. They are a modified version of a prostration. People would fully prostrate themselves upon the ground or floor when entering the presence of an idol, divinized emperor, and eventually lesser princes and officials. This, along with other pagan and civil ceremonial and etiquette gestures, entered the church's liturgical rituals once the church became legally free in the early fourth century. Previously these gestures had been too closely associated with the cult of emperor worship. (See *Catholic Customs and Traditions*, Greg Dues, Twenty-Third Publications, 1992.)

11
ON THE
WINDOW SILL
WITH EUTYCHUS
Bored with Holy Things

Background Notes

Since most teens were baptized as infants, they did not come into the Christ-centered mystery of life and church by way of a clear-cut fundamental decision. This is pretty much the way it has always been. During the first generations of Christianity, it seems that when adults turned to the "new way" of Jesus, it was common that their families, too, were baptized. Infants, toddlers, children, and adolescents were at least on the fringes of early eucharistic assemblies, now called "Mass," while the adults were more involved in what was happening. We can imagine their gathering very much like today's weekend Mass, probably with a little more informality in these ancient house-churches. Less attention was paid to exact time or length of the assembly. There also seemed to be more freedom in coming and going.

There is no reason to think that tendencies on the part of teens today to disengage from formal religion was unheard of in early Christianity. In fact, Scripture provides us with a precious description of a first-generation Mass during which a teen, Eutychus, got caught being bored with the church's liturgy!

Preparation

Make sure the Scripture reading is rehearsed. Prepare copies of the concluding litany.

Time to Listen

Leader (setting the context): The early followers of Jesus met in homes during the evening of what we now call Saturday. Weekdays were measured from sundown to sundown. Therefore, Saturday (Sabbath) evening was already Sunday. It was exciting when one of the apostles visited, more exciting probably for the adults. Scripture tells us about a young person who didn't seem to have been as excited as the grown-ups! Listen to this reading from the Acts of the Apostles, 20:7-12.

Reader 1: On the first day of the week, when we met to break bread, Paul was holding a discussion with them; since he intended to leave the next day, he continued speaking until midnight. There were many lamps in the room upstairs where we were meeting.

Reader 2: A young man named Eutychus, who was sitting in the window, began to sink off into a deep sleep while Paul talked still longer. Overcome by sleep, he fell to the ground three floors below and was picked up dead.

Reader 3: But Paul went down, and bending over him took him into his arms, and said, "Do not be alarmed, for his life is in him." Then Paul went upstairs, and after he had broken bread and eaten, he continued to converse with them until dawn; then he left. Meanwhile they had taken the boy away alive and were not a little comforted.

Response

Follow this reading with a centering exercise. Invite the teens to close their eyes, to imagine being at Mass, to sink into Eutychus's mood, to sit with him on the window sill, so to speak. Do they feel a kinship with Eutychus? When does this usually happen? At which parts of the Mass? How do they feel when this happens? What do they do when they feel this way?

REFLECTION SHEET

After this centering exercise, you might encourage further discussion. Why is it possible to feel bored even though such wonderful mysteries are unfolding?

Challenge the teens to compare their attitude toward going to church to-day and their attitude when they were children; for example, during the year of their First Communion. Why do these changes in attitudes happen?

Review some information about stages of faith taken from earlier prayer assemblies in this book.

Assembly Prayer
(Prepare an antiphonal litany similar to the following.)

Side 1: Jesus said: "I call you friends."

Side 2: Jesus, I will make the effort to stay close to you just as I do with my other friends.

Side 1: Friends like to spend time with each other.

Side 2: Jesus, I will deliberately spend some time with you each week. I will try to do this by going to Mass.

Side 1: Friends like to talk to each other.

Side 2: Jesus, I will talk to you each day and listen to you, too. I will pay attention to your words during Mass.

Side 1: Friends like to share food and drink with each other.

Side 2: Jesus, I plan to sit at table with you each week, sharing the holy bread and cup which is yourself.

12
HALLOWEEN
The Witches and Goblins within Us

Background Notes

This assembly begins with information about the origin of popular Halloween traditions. It concludes with an activity and prayer related to three moods, or patterns of behavior, symbolized by three jack-o'-lanterns.

A high percentage of young people, along with the catechists and youth ministers who have frequent contact with them, come from some kind of dysfunctional family background. They have been influenced by patterns of substance abuse, emotional rigidity, religious extremism, or different kinds of physical and even sexual abuse. A prayer assembly like this is a creative way of releasing in a non-threatening way some of the tensions experienced by individuals in your group.

Catechetics and youth ministry of all kinds can be and in fact should be healing ministries. This does not imply that parish personnel and volunteers should attempt to function in a professional role that is not theirs. They might, however, make available information about confidential opportunities for the young people to share their stories and feelings.

Preparation

Have the young people prepare three jack-o'-lanterns. The faces of one

should be obviously sad; another, angry; and a third, happy. Other moods might be included and written into the assembly. (If there is opportunity, the teens might prepare three *batches* of jack-o'-lanterns.) Some of the young people might prepare paper masks that symbolize the negative attitudes that young people sometimes act out (see author's *Seasonal Prayer Services for Teenagers,* Twenty-Third Publications, 1991). During this preparation, invite the young people to discuss among themselves the moods they are trying to express in the carving and drawing. Encourage them to compete in the grotesqueness and boldness of their creations.

Decorate the assembly area with these jack-o'-lanterns and masks. Before the prayer assembly begins, turn all the "faces" away from the young people.

Volunteers prepare the following readings ahead of time.

Prepare the prayer poster for the Assembly Prayer.

Time to Listen

(Note: These first readings narrate the history and meaning of Halloween customs. They might be included in the preparation time of this prayer assembly, with Narrators 5, 6, and 7 being more directly related to Scripture and prayer.)

Narrator 1: The celebration of Halloween is not directly connected to our Catholic Christian beliefs. Only the name is, taken from the holy day, "Feast of All Saints," which occurs the next day. In the old English language, the eve of All Saints was called "All Hallows Eve," or Halloween. Halloween customs go back to the Celtic people in Britain and Ireland during pre-Christian times. In those ancient times, around November 1, the burning of fires marked the beginning of a new year and the beginning of the season of winter.

Narrator 2: Those people believed that demons, witches, the souls of the dead, and all kinds of evil spirits roamed the world on this night. These creatures of the dark greeted their special season of darkness, the winter season of long nights and early dark evenings, by scaring people, playing mean tricks on them. In the simple beliefs of the people, these creatures of the dark wanted to take them into their kingdom.

Narrator 3: People bought their safety by bribing these creatures of the dark with sweets. Another method of self-protection was to dress like them and roam around without being recognized by these creatures. People still do this today. We wear horrible masks of demons, witches, ghosts, and monsters. And we roam from house to house, sometimes playing pranks, demanding treats with the threat, "Trick or treat!"

Narrator 4: The pumpkin "ghosts," or jack-o'-lanterns, with a burning candle inside, may have come from the Halloween-New Year fires of ancient times. Most probably, however, they came from Irish traditions. Children carved faces on potatoes, turnips, or squash, putting a candle inside to add to the festivities of the night.

Narrator 5: It is all right to enjoy these ancient pagan and earthy festivities because they are wonderfully human. Our Christian faith, however, adds a positive dimension to this time of the year. Tension between dark and light, for example, is very much part of our Scriptures and worship. In fact, Jesus said: "I am the light of the world. Whoever follows me will not walk in darkness, but will have the light of life" (John 8:12).

Narrator 6: Jesus also said that *we* are light: "Your light must shine before others, that they may see your good deeds and glorify your heavenly Father" (Matthew 5:16). How do *we* come across to our friends, family, and people around us? How does *our light* shine on others?

(The *sad* jack-o'-lanterns and masks are turned toward the assembly. Or one is placed on the Prayer Table. Wait until laughter and other reactions die down, then continue.)

Is our light being disfigured by the witches, goblins, demons, and ghosts of our sadness, hurt, frustrations, despair, and depression? Is our light being dimmed by feelings that nobody likes us ... that we aren't as good as others? These moods prevent us from having a positive influence on others.

Narrator 7: (The *angry* jack-o'-lanterns are turned toward the assembly or placed on the Prayer Table.) Is our light being disfigured by the witches, goblins, demons, and ghosts of unjustified anger? ... by our selfishness? ... by our jealousies ... our hostilities? ... our sullenness? These attitudes will have a negative influence on our relationships with others.

Response

Allow some time for reflection and for the young people to discuss causes of negative feelings. You might invite a speaker to talk about some of the support groups available to young people, such as Al-a-Teen.

Assembly Prayer
(The *happy* jack-o'-lanterns, in a prominent place, are turned toward the congregation or placed on the Prayer Table.)

Let us pray.
Lord, make us happy and give us peace.

Take away the witches,
goblins, demons, and ghosts of all
that is not good within us.
Give us strength to leave our addictions.
Give us the courage to maintain our emotional health
and take care of ourselves.
Help our good light to shine from within us,
shining toward all who come in contact with us. Amen.

(Continue with spontaneous prayer.)

13
THANKSGIVING
Different Ways of Knowing God

Background Notes

Each year is full of all kinds of critical transitions. Some of these are associated with the change of natural seasons and others with the change of liturgical seasons. (For more prayer services celebrating these transitions, see my *Seasonal Prayer Services for Teenagers*, Twenty-Third Publications, 1991.) For example, during the season of autumn teens return to classes after the (usually) wonderful free times of summer. Soon after that, another transition takes place as nature changes from the lush greens so evident during spring and summer to the red, golds, yellow, bronzes, and browns of autumn. In the fields throughout the northern hemisphere, harvest replaces planting, germinating, and growing. Grains and fruit replace delicate buds and blossoms of the months before.

There are seasonal transitions in human life, too, as we go through different stages of faith and human development. Adolescence is one such critical transition. Teens struggle with new challenges; relationships take over the center of their life. Besides beginning a searching phase in their faith, they also have to struggle with new ways of knowing things. This prayer assembly celebrates the wonder of these new ways of knowing as teens, along with their families, prepare to celebrate a joyful Thanksgiving Day.

Adolescents gradually move from a reliance on concrete, imaginative processes of childhood to a more abstract process of thinking and learning. They do not make this transition *suddenly or as a group,* however. In any one group, individual teens will be "all over the ball park." For example, when they are invited to celebrate the presence of God in nature around them, they will interpret it according to where they are in their own journey of human development. Obviously, they are no longer little children excited about and satisfied with repeating seasonal rituals and activities, such as making crude turkeys in arts and crafts or acting out the perennial drama of Pilgrims and Native Americans. Nor have they arrived at adult forms of learning, remembering, and commitment. They are in a very acceptable in-between stage.

In this prayer assembly teens are invited to consider different ways of knowing the mystery of God and different ways of talking about this mystery as they continue to make a transition to a more adult faith.

Preparation

Obtain a copy of Leo Leoni's *Frederick* from the library or bookstore. Prepare a reflection sheet. Have volunteers prepare the readings below, which are taken from this book. (Note: This book is so short that it could easily be read in its entirety for this assembly. If not, the selection provided would be sufficient.)

In preparation for a response and prayer, engage the teens in discussion. Briefly explain the change that is taking place in their patterns of learning, making use of the Background Notes, above. How have they felt the transition from a reliance on the concrete, imaginative processes of childhood to a more abstract process of thinking and learning? Discuss with them the rituals, games, and visuals that were so important in their childhood. You might list these on the board or wall paper. Don't hurry the discussion.

Explain that there will be two entirely different readings for this prayer assembly. Invite them to enjoy the mystery of God as it is revealed so differently in each of the readings.

Time to Listen

Leader: Leo Leoni's children's book *Frederick* is a delightful story of a field mouse who, instead of collecting food supplies as the others do, collects memories of the warm sun, colors, and descriptive words for the cold months ahead. In a final poem, *Frederick* gives credit to four field mice in the sky for all the wonderful things of creation.

Reader 1:   Who scatters snowflakes? Who melts the ice?

Who spoils the weather? Who makes it nice?

Who grows the four-leaf clovers in June?

Who dims the daylight? Who lights the moon?

Reader 2: Four little field mice who live in the sky.
Four little field mice ... like you and I.
One is the Springmouse who turns on the showers.
Then comes the Summer who paints in the flowers.
The Fallmouse is next with walnuts and wheat.
And Winter is last ... with little cold feet.

Reader 3: Aren't we lucky the seasons are four?
Think of a year with one less ... or one more!

REFLECTION SHEET

Encourage sharing. How do simple stories preserve profound insights into what is real? What stories from their childhood do the teens remember that do this? Does the story of Frederick still speak to them, or do they now consider it too juvenile?

Regardless of their feelings about the story, what precious memories have they collected from this past year that they are grateful for this Thanksgiving? Encourage the teens to share some of these and to list them on large prayer sheets for posting.

Time to Listen

(Continue now with the following Scripture reading.)

Reader 4: The Book of Deuteronomy in the Bible says: "When you have come into the land that the Lord your God is giving you as an inheritance,

and you possess it and settle in it, you shall take some of the first of all the fruit of the ground, which you harvest from the land that the Lord your God is giving you, and you shall put it in a basket and go to the place that the Lord your God will choose as a dwelling for his name. You shall go to the priest who is in the office at that time, and say to him... 'I bring the first of the fruit of the ground that you, O Lord, have given me.' ...then you...shall celebrate with all the bounty that the Lord your God has given to you and to your house" (26:1-2, 10-11).

REFLECTION SHEET

How are both readings (from *Frederick* and from Scripture) similar? Different? What reading spoke most clearly to them? Why? Was the faith of our childhood just as correct as now?

The apostle Paul shares this insight with us: "When I was a child, I spoke like a child, I thought like a child, I reasoned like a child; when I became an adult, I put an end to childish ways..." (1 Corinthians 13:11). In what ways do the teens feel that they are in this transition to adulthood?

Assembly Prayer

> It is good to give thanks to the Lord,
> to sing praises to your name, O Most High;
> to declare your steadfast love in the morning,
> and your faithfulness by night,
> to the music of the lute and the harp,
> to the melody of the lyre.
> For you, O Lord, have made me glad by your work;
> at the works of your hands I sing for joy.
> How great are your works, O Lord!
>
> *Psalm 92*

(Encourage the young people to continue with their own spontaneous praise and prayers of thanksgiving.)

14
ADVENT
Celebrating the Cycle of Time

Background Notes

The church year does not have an exact beginning or end; it is like a circle. Advent comes first only in a popular sense, a result of the need to begin the official church books at some definite point. The mystery of Jesus' birth is a good starting point for the church year, though the actual choice of this significant date has a complicated history.

The beginning of Advent and a new church year offers an opportunity to share with the young people some creative insights into the mystery of the cycle of time. Our rich Catholic Christian liturgical traditions, and popular ones, too, are appreciated best in the context of their earthy origins. Many of them evolved from the observation and then the celebration of the ever-hopeful repetition of the yearly cycle, especially the tension between light and darkness.

There are four pivotal points in the yearly cycle of time, each marking a moment in this tension between light and dark. At two of these points, the sun is directly above Earth's equator, and the length of days and nights is equal. This is called an *equinox* (Latin, "equal night") and they take place on March 20 or 21 and September 22 or 23. The March equinox marks the beginning of spring and is called the vernal (Latin, "of spring") equinox. A season for new life in planting and growing begins. It is the pivotal point that sets the date for Easter (the first Sunday after the first full moon after the spring equinox), and therefore the season of Lent that prepares for Easter. The September equinox begins the season of autumn. It begins a time for harvesting what the new life has brought. It is also a preparation for a kind of dying throughout nature and the beginning of colder weather.

Balancing these two pivotal points are the summer solstice and the winter solstice (Latin, "sun stands"), as planet Earth slants as far as possible toward the sun—June 20 or 21 (beginning of summer)—giving us in the temperate zones the longest days of the year. Or as far away as possible from the sun—December 21 or 22 (beginning of winter)—giving us the longest nights.

No particular religious tradition flows from the summer solstice, but almost all of our Christmas traditions depend upon the winter solstice. As the nights lengthened in the temperate zones and the cold of winter approached, people of ancient times would bring green branches into their humble homes, a reminder of warmer times when the world was full of the green of life. The increasing dark of night also brought out the need for burning lights for practical purposes, eventually giving rise to a pre-Christian Festival of Lights. As Christianity spread to the northern countries of Europe, these ancient traditions received new meaning from faith in the coming of Jesus Christ, *the* light of the world, whose coming brings a new light of salvation into the darkness of sin. His birth began to be celebrated at the moment of the winter solstice when the "unconquerable sun" began winning out again over the dark, with daylight increasing from that moment.

So, from this tension of light and dark came our delightful traditions of the Advent Wreath, Christmas lights, Christmas trees, and even the celebration of the Nativity itself.

Preparation

If possible, plan for this prayer assembly weeks ahead. Encourage the teens to note the change in light and dark, with the sun setting earlier each day by a minute or so. You might chart this on a posterboard or mural. Have the teens get this information from the newspaper, meteorology reports, or science books; it is important that they appreciate the cycle of time and tension between light and dark.

Bring in a globe, and demonstrate the relation of Earth and sun and how this relationship affects our religious traditions. Also, have some seasonal decorations such as lights and greenery and an Advent Wreath displayed. Obtain a string of Christmas lights, the kind that allows bulbs to burn separately. Light one more each day.

Assign and prepare the readings below.

Response

Gather around an Advent Wreath, candles unlit, room semi-dark. Begin by enthusiastically wishing the teens a "Happy New Year!" There will prob-

ably be some corrections or objections. Reply that this prayer assembly celebrates the mystery of a new church year. Discuss briefly the seasonal relationship between light and dark explained in the Background Notes, and then continue with the readings.

Time to Listen

Leader (setting the context): Primitive humans marveled at the grand lights in the sky. The greater one ruled the day and the lesser one ruled the night (Genesis 1:16). They noticed the regular cycle of these two lights: the moon and the sun. Guided by the lights' regular appearances, they celebrated memorable events that had happened in their clans or tribes.

Reader 1: And God said, "Let there be lights in the dome of the sky to separate the day from the night; and let them be for signs and for seasons and for days and years, and let there be lights in the dome of the sky to give light upon Earth." And it was so. God made the two great lights—the greater light to rule the day and the lesser light to rule the night—and the stars.

Reader 2: And God said, "Let there be lights in the dome of the sky to give light upon Earth, to rule over the day and over the night, and to separate the light from the darkness." And God saw that it was good. And there was evening and there was morning, the fourth day (Genesis 1:14-19).

Leader: People noticed that there is a seasonal cycle that repeats according to a regular and accurate law of nature. They celebrated the beginning of these cycles: a new year in the ever-repeating cycle of time. The vernal, or spring, equinox (approximately March 22) was a popular day to begin a new year. Celtic people in Britain and Ireland celebrated the end of October as the beginning of a new year, giving rise to some of our Halloween traditions. Our January 1 was set for the Roman Empire by Julius Caesar in 45 B.C.E.

People who followed the Way of Jesus remembered that he spoke of light and dark.

Reader 3: Again Jesus spoke to them, saying, "I am the light of the world. Whoever follows me will never walk in darkness but will have the light of life" (John 8:12).

Leader: Eventually Christians began to celebrate the birth of their Lord and Light at that time of the year when light once again begins to win out over darkness. This was at the winter solstice, approximately December 25. They preceded this with a short preparation period called Advent, marking the beginning of a new church year.

Reader 3: The people who walked in darkness have seen a great light; those who lived in a land of deep darkness—on them light has shone (Isaiah 9:2).

(Light the candles on the Advent Wreath and the string of Christmas lights.)

Assembly Prayer
(Responsorial Psalm from Christmas Mass at Dawn)

All: A light will shine on us this day: the Lord is born for us.

Leader: The Lord is king; let Earth rejoice;

let the many isles be glad.

The heavens proclaim his justice,

and all peoples see his glory.

All: A light will shine on us this day: the Lord is born for us.

Leader: Light dawns for the just;

and gladness, for the upright of heart.

Be glad in the Lord, you just,

and give thanks to his holy name.

All: A light will shine on us this day: the Lord is born for us.

(Conclude with spontaneous prayers about the "dark" and "light" in our lives.)

15
LENT
A Crucial Moment—Part One

(Note: This prayer assembly celebrates the experiences of those who witnessed the tragic death of Jesus. The following one [16] then celebrates the time after the cross and resurrection, when the events had been put into perspective through the power of their faith and religious experience. You might prefer to divide these assemblies differently, possibly taking a different character each week of Lent and celebrate the "before" and "after" for each character in the same assembly. Finally, Prayer Assembly 17 is a simplified version and can serve as a substitute for the previous ones.)

Background Notes

The most crucial moment in the history of salvation has always been identified by the symbol of the cross. In fact, "crucial" comes from the Latin *crux*, meaning "cross." A crucial moment is, therefore, a cross, or pivotal, moment. The cross was never a sign of defeat. From the dawn of Christianity it has been a sign rather of commitment, decision, and victory—first for Jesus and then for every person marked with the cross in baptism.

The cross divides "time before" from "time after"—first for those who experienced that historical moment outside the walls of Jerusalem and now for us who experience it anew.

This prayer assembly encourages the teens to identify their own crucial moments, to reflect on them, and to grow spiritually through them.

Preparation

Select teens to portray the gospel characters who witnessed the crucifixion of Jesus (see narratives, below). These parts should be well rehearsed because they form the bulk of the assembly and will speak to the hearts of the teens gathered to get inside the story.

Atmosphere is very important. Darkness should prevail as much as possible. A crude cross, full size (made of cheap boards), should be in a prominent place and spotlighted. The "cross characters," seated close by—some on the floor and others on high stools—make use of this light. The teens should surround these "cross characters" as closely as possible, like a theater in the round.

A leader introduces the prayer session by explaining the derivation of the word "crucial" and the meaning of a crucial moment. See Background Notes, above.

The leader continues by leading the young people in a centering exercise or fantasy ... taking them to Golgotha. How do they feel as they experience the crucifixion of Jesus? The first verses of the spiritual "Were You There?" would help set the mood.

Time to Listen

Narrator 1: It is one year after the death and resurrection of Jesus. His friends have reunited for a time. They remember the intense moment of the cross and his resurrection. First they will share with us their experience of witnessing the agony of the cross. At another time they will testify to the change that took place in them when the cross blended with the resurrection of Jesus. The people you will hear are those mentioned in the gospels. Their testimony is based on the Scriptures. We invite you to get close to their experiences. Let them become yours.

Mary Magdalene: I am Mary from Magdala. After Jesus drove evil spirits from me and then befriended me, I stayed close to him and learned so much from him. I grew in love for him. Then came the cross. I was there. The hands that reached out to me in love and understanding were nailed to wood. I was drained of all hope. I was depressed as never before to see my friend suffer so much.

Salome: I am Salome, the wife of Zebedee. My two sons, James and John, were apostles of Jesus. I came from Galilee with Mary of Magdala and another woman called Mary, the mother of James and Joses. We took care of the needs of Jesus and his apostles, such as the cooking and washing, and supported them out of our own resources. I, too, was at the cross, watching from a distance. I saw the soldiers fight over Jesus' clothes after they stripped him. I saw the sarcastic notice they nailed above his head: "This is

Jesus, the Nazarean, King of the Jews." Jesus did not die alone. Two thieves were executed with him, one on his left and one on his right. I was terribly worried about my sons. Would they be arrested, too, and put to death? One of my sons, John, was standing so close to the place of execution that Jesus could talk to him.

Mary, Wife of Clopas: I am the wife of Clopas and the mother of James and Joses. I was at the cross with Mary from Magdala and Salome. What really hurt me was the way the people insulted and taunted Jesus. He had done nothing but good during his life. But they yelled at him: "So you are the one who was going to destroy the temple and rebuild it in three days? Why don't you save yourself? Come down off that cross if you are God's Son!" Even our religious leaders, the chief priests, scribes, and elders insulted him, saying: "He saved others but he cannot save himself! He relied on God; let God rescue him now if he wants to." Even the thieves dying with Jesus seemed to mock him. I thought to myself: "What good can come of this tragedy? How can people be so cruel?" I felt I would never trust anyone again.

Mary, Mother of Jesus: I am Mary, Jesus' mother. I was always so proud of him. There was a brightness and joy whenever he was around, first in our home and then in the crowds and in other people's homes. I was there at the cross when they put him to death. What I felt most was the terrible darkness from noon on. It was noisy and frightening. Everything I had lived for was being destroyed. My dreams for my child were shattered. When Jesus was a baby, the holy man Simeon told me my child was destined to be the downfall and the rise of many. He would be a person that many people would oppose. Simeon also predicted that my own heart would be pierced. I never imagined how painful that piercing would be until I looked into the dying face of my son. Then Jesus looked at me and seemed to nod toward John who was there with me. He said: "Woman, there is your son." Then he said to John: "There is your mother." A couple of hours later they put the body of Jesus into my arms for the last time.

John: I am John, a very close friend of Jesus. I was there, close to the cross. During all that shouting and darkness I watched as the soldiers made sure he was dead. One of them stuck a spear into his side and the last of his blood flowed out. I stood there looking at him—wondering if this was the end of all our hopes. I wondered, too, about friendship. Is this the price of friendship? To stay close to a friend in the most terrible of times? Even though it hurts so much?

Peter: I am Peter, the one Jesus called a "rock." But on the day of the cross I was nothing but a soft sponge. The rest of you didn't even know that I saw the crucifixion—from where I was hiding a good distance off. I could hear my master cry out: "My God, my God, why have you forsaken me?" Just hours before, I saw that same cry in his eyes—but then it was directed at me. When I was given the chance to stand up and defend Jesus, I denied that I even knew him. I was scared that I would be arrested next because I was known as the leader of the group. Jesus had warned me that I would weaken, but I was too proud. Later his eyes told me just how weak I was. But as I stood there with the cross in the distance I wondered: Did Jesus expect too much of me? It wasn't so hard being a "rock" when the crowds cheered Jesus and respected me. But this crowd on Golgotha was not the cheering kind. And I was afraid to be associated with the victim.

Simon the Cyrenian: I am Simon from Cyrene. I didn't want to be at the cross, but I was in the wrong place at the wrong time. Jesus was so weak from the whipping and crowning with thorns that he couldn't carry the crosspiece by himself. The soldiers drafted me to carry it. I didn't appreciate that. I was afraid to get mixed up with the crazy things going on. Put it this way, I didn't want to get involved. It wasn't any of my business.

Response

(If possible, repeat the first two verses of "Were You There?")

Narrator 2 (to the assembly of teens): You were there, too. Each of you has stood at the cross. You will stand there many times again. You stand there when someone doesn't like you ... or hurts you ... or when you are confused by a terrible turn of events. You stand at the cross when you are sick ... when you are depressed. Each of you has your own cross ... your own crucial moment. Your cross may look different than the cross of your friends ... but it weighs the same because for each it is the cross of Jesus. You have an important choice: your cross ... your crucial moment ... can defeat you ... or with faith it can become a crucial moment of victory ... and new life.

Narrator 3: Close your eyes ... think of the worst thing now bothering you ... imagine yourself at the cross of Jesus... blend yourself into his suffering and death ...

Narrator 4: Come forward now ... gain strength from the cross ... touch the cross for a moment ... press into the wood your own suffering ... your confusions ... your depression ... your fears ... your sin ...

(One by one, or in pairs, the teens approach the cross and touch or hold it, staying there a while. This takes some time, depending on the number present and their emotions. This prayer assembly should be scheduled in such a way that this response does not seem rushed. Recorded music should be played, or songs sung. End the prayer service in silence.)

(Important Note: If the next prayer session will not be celebrated this season, make sure that its ending is incorporated into this prayer session so that the experience ends on the positive note intended.)

16
LENT
A Crucial Moment—Part Two

Background Notes

See Background Notes from the previous assembly (15). This prayer session is designed to follow that one. There the young people met the friends and mother of Jesus as they testified to their experience of the crucifixion, the *crucial* moment of all history. At the end the young people were invited to come to grips with their own crucial moments.

Now the young people once again meet with the friends and mother of Jesus. This time, however, they hear testimony of the personal consequences of the death and resurrection of Jesus, after the events have been put into perspective through the power of their faith and continuing religious experiences.

As mentioned in the previous prayer assembly, you might prefer a different division, possibly taking a different character each week of Lent and celebrate the "before" and "after" in the same session.

Preparation

Assign the parts of the gospel characters who witnessed the crucifixion and resurrection of Jesus (see narratives, below). These parts should be well rehearsed because they form the bulk of the assembly and the teens need to get inside the story and make it personal.

Atmosphere is very important. Once again a large, full-size crude cross, (made of cheap boards) should be in a prominent place and spotlighted. The atmosphere should be changed from the previous session, however. The cross, for example, might be decorated with signs of life and joy.

Make copies of the closing antiphonal prayer.

If funds are available, purchase inexpensive cross pins or medallions for a closing investiture ritual.

Once again, "cross characters" are seated near the cross in such a way that they can communicate well with the assembly.

A leader begins the session with an imagination exercise: What do you think happened to the gospel characters once they experienced the resurrection of Jesus? If you had been in their sandals, so to speak, what changes do you think would have occurred in your own life and behavior?

Time to Listen

Narrator 1: It is still a year after the death and resurrection of Jesus and his friends, still gathered together, remember the intense moment of the cross *as it blends with the intense moment of Jesus' resurrection.* They will testify to the change that took place in them. The people you will hear are those mentioned in the gospels. Their testimony is based on the Scriptures. We will understand our own experience of the cross better if we become part of their experience.

Mary Magdalene: I am Mary from Magdala, from whom Jesus drove the evil spirits and then made me his friend. How quickly that terrible moment of the cross passed! Three days later, in the garden by the tomb, I met Jesus again. He looked at me and spoke my name: "Mary!" He was no longer dead. He was still with me! To this day my heart beats fast whenever I talk to others about what happened to me. And I always seem to be talking about it! The cross of death has turned into a cross of life for Jesus—and for me.

Salome: I am Salome, the wife of Zebedee and the mother of James and John, apostles of Jesus. I ministered to the needs of Jesus and his community of apostles, traveling with them until the end. I did it because Jesus was so important to my sons. Now I feel the presence of Jesus in every community I become part of. Now I minister to the needs of widows, orphans, the homeless, and the hungry. Ever since I experienced Jesus still among us, I feel his presence in every person that needs my help. I see his face in their faces. I feel again his agony in their agony. And I feel his resurrection in their relief and joy when I help them.

Mary, Wife of Clopas: I am the wife of Clopas and the mother of James and Joses. So much happened so quickly. But then the excitement quieted down. My husband and I had so little to give to the families who joined the new way that Jesus taught, so we opened our simple home to them. Believers met there every Sabbath night for the sharing of bread and cup. We felt the presence of Jesus very deeply in those moments.

Mary, Mother of Jesus: I am Mary, Jesus' mother. I have never felt as close to my son as I do now. Not even when I held him as a baby to nurse him. He is no longer just mine. He belongs to everyone. My heart was pierced with sorrow, standing at the cross, but now it is pierced with joy. Day after day hundreds more reach out to him as Lord and brother. And I feel like the mother of a family already too numerous to count!

John: I am John. I always considered myself the closest friend of Jesus. But nothing can compare to the friendship I feel for him now. I used to sit close to him and treasure his words. Now my heart bursts with his love, and power, and spirit. Every time I preach his words I end up talking about love. Love was the focus of his life and preaching. When I remember the cross, I remember his love. That moment of agony has become the moment of total love.

Peter: I am Peter, still head of this new community of believers. Jesus called me "the rock." When I met him on the third day after the cross, I began to realize finally what he wanted of me. I had been so weak and wishy-washy. Then one day after his resurrection to new life, he looked at me again and asked: "Peter, do you love me?" All of my past failures rushed to my memory. Here was someone I had denied and he was still reaching out to me. I answered with all my heart: "Yes, Lord, you know that I love you!" Three times he asked the same question; three times I gave the same answer. Each time he said: "Feed my lambs!" All I want to do now is to be a rock of security to others who are as weak and frightened as I was then.

Simon the Cyrenian: I am Simon from Cyrene. I had helped Jesus carry his cross. I walked away from Golgotha carrying a different cross than I carried hours before. I had never heard of Jesus. There on that hill I witnessed the death of an innocent man. The life that flowed out of his body seemed to flow into mine. I came down from the hill carrying the cross of victory. And I was ready when the others testified that he had been raised from the dead. I, perhaps more than anyone else, understood the words of Jesus they shared with me after the resurrection: "Unless you pick up the cross and follow me, you cannot have life in me." I and my sons, Alexander and Rufus, now remember Jesus in the breaking of bread and the sharing of the cup. The cross has truly been a crucial moment for me.

Response

Narrator 2: Jesus is raised from the dead. His cross is now a cross of victory. You, too, can reach out and be touched by his victory. Your cross of suffering can become a cross of victory. Your crucial moment, the worst thing bothering you, can turn into victory!

Narrator 3: Come forward again. Once more, touch the cross for a moment. Be grateful for the gift of faith. Feel close to the Lord, still present, your caring and powerful companion.

(One by one, or in pairs, the teens approach the cross and touch it. Joyful music should play during this time or a joyful songs sung. After all have gone to the cross, the session ends with this antiphonal prayer:)

Assembly Prayer

Leader: Let us pray about our crucial moments. *Before*—we were afraid.

All: Now—through the power of your cross of victory, we will have confidence.

Leader: Before—we went to pieces when someone didn't like us.

All: Now—through the power of your cross of victory, we will continue to love even when we are not loved.

Leader: Before—we were timid when our beliefs were ridiculed.

All: Now—through the power of your cross of victory, we will stand firm in our faith.

Leader: Before—we turned inward to satisfy our own needs.

All: Now—through the power of your cross of victory, we will reach outward to meet the needs of others.

Leader: Before—we were often ashamed of our religious convictions.

All: Now—through the power of your cross of victory, we will be proud of our faith.

Leader: Before—we were swayed by the latest fad.

All: Now—through the power of your cross of victory, we will search out your will instead.

Leader: Before—we often betrayed and denied you by our behavior.

All: Now—through the power of your cross of victory, we will proclaim you by faith and a life of love.

Conclude with an investiture ritual. With music playing, invest each teen with an inexpensive cross pin or medallion. If this is not possible, invite the teens to stand for a minute with arms outstretched in a cruciform gesture. Or, slowly and ritually trace a cross on the forehead of each, as in baptism.

17
LENT
A Crucial Moment
(Simplified Version)

(Note: This prayer assembly serves as a substitute for the two previous ones, which were more lengthy and involved. The same theme is celebrated, using only the introduction, which sets the context, and the concluding response activities and prayer.)

Background Notes

The most *crucial* moment in the history of salvation has always been identified by the symbol of the cross. In fact, "crucial" comes from the Latin *crux*, meaning "cross." A crucial moment is, therefore, a cross, or pivotal, moment. The cross was never a sign of defeat. From the dawn of Christianity it has been a sign rather of commitment, decision, and victory—first for Jesus and then for every person marked with the cross in baptism.

The cross divides "time before" from "time after"—first for those who experienced that historical moment outside the walls of Jerusalem and now for us who experience it anew.

This prayer assembly encourages the teens to identify their own crucial moments, to reflect on them, and to grow spiritually through them.

Preparation

Prepare copies of the closing antiphonal prayer.

Purchase inexpensive cross pins or medallions for a closing investiture ritual.

The assembly area should feature a crude cross, full size (made of cheap boards). Subdued lighting. Joyful decorations should be ready outside of the viewing area for the final part of this prayer assembly.

Response

Introduce the prayer session by explaining the derivation of the word "crucial" and the meaning of a crucial moment. (See Background Notes, above.)

An optional introduction would be to read the gospel passion in narrative form as is done on Passion (Palm) Sunday and Good Friday.

The leader continues by leading the young people in a centering exercise or fantasy ... taking them to Golgotha. How do they feel as they experience the crucifixion of Jesus? The first two verses of "Were You There?" would help set the mood.

Narrator 1 (to the assembly of teens): You were there, too. Each of you has stood at the cross. You will stand there many times again. You stand there when someone doesn't like you ... or hurts you ... or when you are confused by a terrible turn of events. You stand at the cross when you are sick ... when you are depressed. Each of you has your own cross ... your own crucial moment. Your cross may look different than the cross of your friends ... but it weighs the same because for each it is the cross of Jesus. You have an important choice: your cross ... your crucial moment ... can defeat you ... or with faith it can become a crucial moment of victory ... and new life.

Narrator 2: Close your eyes ... think of the worst thing now bothering you ... imagine yourself at the cross of Jesus ... blend yourself into his suffering and death.

Narrator 3: Come forward now ... gain strength from the cross ... touch the cross for a moment ... press your own suffering into the wood ... your confusions ... your depression ... your fears ... your sin.

(One by one, or in pairs, the teens approach the cross and touch or hold it, staying there a while. This takes some time, depending on the numbers present and their emotions. This prayer session should be scheduled in such a way that this response does not seem rushed. Recorded music should be played, or songs sung. When all the teens have been to the cross, quickly change the atmosphere of the assembly area. The cross, for example, might be decorated now with signs of life and joy.)

Narrator 1: Jesus is raised from the dead. His cross is now a cross of victory. You, too, can reach out and be touched by his victory. Your cross of suffering can become a cross of victory. Your crucial moment, the worst thing bothering you, can turn into victory!

Narrator 2: Come forward again. Touch again the cross for just a moment. Be grateful for the strength that comes from your gift of faith. Feel close to the Lord, still present, your caring and powerful companion.

(For a second time, one by one, or in pairs, the teens approach the cross. Joyful music should play during this time or a joyful songs sung. After all have gone to the cross, the session ends with an antiphonal prayer.)

Leader: Let us pray about our crucial moments. *Before*—we were afraid.

All: Now—through the power of your cross of victory, we will have confidence.

Leader: Before—we went to pieces when someone didn't like us.

All: Now—through the power of your cross of victory, we will continue to love even when we are not loved.

Leader: Before—we were timid when our beliefs were ridiculed.

All: Now—through the power of your cross of victory, we will stand firm in our faith.

Leader: Before—we turned inward to satisfy our own needs.

All: Now—through the power of your cross of victory, we will reach outward to meet the needs of others.

Leader: *Before*—we were often ashamed of our religious convictions.

All: *Now*—through the power of your cross of victory, we will be proud of our faith.

Leader: *Before*—we were swayed by the latest fad.

All: *Now*—through the power of your cross of victory, we will search out your will instead.

Leader: *Before*—we often betrayed and denied you by our behavior.

All: *Now*—through the power of your cross of victory, we will proclaim you by faith and good deeds.

Conclude with an investiture ritual. With music playing, invest each teen with an inexpensive cross pin or medallion. If this is not possible, invite the teens to stand for a minute with arms outstretched in a cruciform gesture. Or, slowly and ritually trace a cross on the forehead of each, as in baptism.

18
EASTER: COME TO THE WATER

Experiencing the Mystery of Baptism

Background Notes

Most teens were baptized as infants. It is important that they experience the mystery of baptism as they struggle with their own faith today. This prayer assembly provides one such experience.

An ancient catechesis on the mystery of baptism comes from Paul's letter to the Romans. In it (quoted in the prayer service, below), Paul likens the baptism experience to going down into a tomb, experiencing a death, then leaving the dead, old stuff behind and rising to a new life with Christ. In this prayer experience, the teens are invited to do the same symbolically—to put into the waters their old self, their sins, whatever needs to be shed. Only then will they rise to new life.

A good time for this prayer experience is the Easter season, especially during a confirmation retreat.

Preparation

Pick a place that is closely associated with baptism: baptismal pool or font. From these waters fill cups, one for each teen. Assign and rehearse the readings.

Response

Invite the teens to sit comfortably around the waters, each holding a cup of the water. Explain that the waters were taken from the baptismal font or pool.

With calming words and with music in the background, invite the teens to center themselves in silence. There are good tapes available with the sounds of water on the sea shore, in a brook, or waterfall.

Leader (setting the context): Many years ago you were carried to the waters of baptism. You were not conscious, however, of the mysteries that fill the waters of baptism. Enjoy those mysteries now.

Reader 1: The apostle Paul says: "Do you not know that all of us who have been baptized into Christ Jesus were baptized into his death? Therefore we have been buried with him by baptism into death, so that, just as Christ was raised from the dead by the glory of the Father, so we too might walk in the newness of life" (Romans 6:3-4).

Reader 2: Paul continues: "For if we have been united with him in a death like his, we will certainly be united with him in a resurrection like his. We know that our old self was crucified with him so that the body of sin might be destroyed, and we might no longer be enslaved to sin. For whoever has died is freed from sin. But if we have died with Christ, we believe that we will also live with him. We know that Christ, being raised from the dead, will never die again; death no longer has dominion over him. The death he died, he died to sin, once for all; but the life he lives, he lives to God. So you also must consider yourselves dead to sin and alive to God in Christ Jesus" (Romans 6:5-11).

Leader (leading the teens into a centering exercise, pausing frequently): We cannot be rebaptized ... but we can go down into the waters again symbolically ... let us do that now ... let us put our old selves into those waters ... become very conscious of the water we are holding ... let our anxieties flow out of you into that water ... let the mistakes we made flow out of us into this water ... mistakes in our relationships ...

Let our sins and bad patterns of living flow out of us into this water ... our patterns of selfishness ... our patterns of addictions ... our patterns of cheating ... our patterns of dishonesty in our actions and words ... let them flow out into this water ... let our confusions flow out of us into this water ... not knowing what choices to make ... not knowing how to relate to our parents and friends ... all our confusions ... let them flow out of us into this water ... let our fears flow out of us into this water ... our fear of the future ... our fear of loneliness ... our fear of death ... let all our fears flow out of us into this water...

Assembly Prayer

Leader: (Allow some time for silence, perhaps with soothing water music playing.) Now let us pour this water into the baptismal font or pool ... pouring out all the negative stuff we put into it ... pouring our old self into the baptismal waters ... feeling free of all that needs to die ... feeling new again in the resurrection of Jesus Christ ... a resurrection that we already enjoy as baptized people.

(Each teen ritually pours their water into the baptismal font as the water music continues for awhile. Afterwards, invite the teens to share their feelings about the experience.)

19
PENTECOST
Reading Signs of the Spirit

Background Notes

Teens disengage themselves more from religious teaching than from a relationship with God. Sometimes we create this situation by overloading them with dry theological notions and detailed catechesis instead of providing opportunities for religious experiences. For example, as teens approach confirmation, it is important that they experience the wonders that gave birth to the church community, the wonders of an exciting Spirit of the living God. These wonders were recorded with symbolic language in Acts 2:1-21 because it was impossible to describe them adequately in words.

This prayer assembly invites the teens to "read the signs" of that most moving, exciting moment among the followers of Jesus. Then they are invited to reflect upon these mysteries as they are evident in their own religious experience.

Preparation

Assign and rehearse the Scripture readings. Prepare in the assembly area a number of candles or lamps that burn with bold flames. Also provide large pieces of red cloth. Some kind of fan will also come in handy.

Time to Listen

Leader (setting the context): For a while the friends and followers of Jesus experienced his continued presence after his resurrection in an overwhelming way. Then he was gone again. They gathered in their favorite place, in the upper room where they had eaten a Last Supper with Jesus, the Upper Room where he had later appeared to them several times after his resurrection.

Peter and John were there. So were James, Andrew, Philip, Thomas, Bartholomew, Matthew, James son of Alphaeus, Simon the Zealot, Judas son of James, and Matthias who had just been chosen to take the place of Judas. There were women there, along with the mother of Jesus, and some of Jesus' family, about a hundred and twenty altogether.

Let us imagine that we are there, too. (Slowly announce the names of all teens present.)

Then something exciting happened.

Reader 1: When the day of Pentecost had come, they were all together in one place. And suddenly from heaven there came a sound like the rush of violent wind, and it filled the entire house where they were sitting.

Reader 2: Divided tongues, as of fire, appeared among them, and a tongue rested on each of them. All of them were filled with the Holy Spirit and began to speak in other languages, as the Spirit gave them ability.

Reader 3: Now there were devout Jews from every nation under heaven living in Jerusalem. And at this sound the crowd gathered and was bewildered, because each one heard them speaking in the native tongue of each.

Amazed and astonished, they asked, "Are not all these who are speaking Galileans? And how is it that we hear, each of us, in our own native language?"

Reader 4: But Peter, standing with the eleven, raised his voice and addressed them, "Men of Judea and all who live in Jerusalem, let this be known to you, and listen to what I say. Indeed, these are not drunk, as you suppose, for it is only nine o'clock in the morning....No, this is what was spoken through the prophet Joel:

> In the last days it will be, God declares,
> that I will pour out my Spirit
> upon all flesh....
> Then everyone who calls on the name of
> the Lord shall be saved (see Acts 2:1-21).

Response

Discuss what the teens heard in this story that was out of the ordinary. What choice of words points to something extraordinary happening? These are *signs:* descriptions of physical things that point to divine mysteries. Make sure that the following signs are mentioned and recorded on a chart:

- sound like the rush of a violent wind
- presence of fire that rested on each of them
- some kind of speaking in other tongues
- acting so high that the people appeared drunk

Once the teens have identified the special signs in the story, challenge them to "read" these signs, discovering layers of meaning, new insights into the mystery of the Spirit of God, and how this Spirit lives in and through them. For example, what is there about a "rush of a violent wind" that says something about the Spirit (moving force, etc.)? Draw attention to the physical symbols in the assembly area: flames and red cloths. Turn on the fan, letting the breeze play with the flames and red cloths.

Divide the teens into groups of 3 for this sharing reflection. At the conclusion, each group is to compose a prayer to the Spirit of God, using ideas from one of the signs or images.

REFLECTION SHEET

What does each of the following *signs* in the Pentecost story say about the Spirit of God?

- sound like the rush of a violent wind
- presence of fire that rested on each of them
- some kind of speaking in other tongues
- acting so high that the people appeared drunk

Compose a prayer to the Spirit, using insights from your shared reflection:

Assembly Prayer

Gather around the Prayer Table. Have Pentecost signs and symbols evident. Invite the teens to direct their prayers to the Spirit. The following is a sample:

> Spirit of the living God,
>   move us to good works
>   when we tend to stay put in our laziness.
> Warm us up when we are spiritually cold.
> Burn in us with a love for others,
>   a love that is your powerful presence.
> When our faith gets boring,
>   put some excitement into our life.
> Make us enthusiastic for good things,
>   make us high for love of you
>   and for love of your people. Amen.

20
COMING HOME AGAIN
An Experience of Reconciliation

Background Notes

Returning home! This is one of the most pleasant human experiences. After a time of separation from loved ones, either a voluntary or forced separation, it feels so good to come back. Especially if the welcome is evident.

It is not uncommon, especially in the past, for religious leaders to describe God in harsh terms, a God who almost seems to seek revenge when people don't quite "toe the mark," as it were. Jesus, who knew God "inside and out" because he is God, tells a different tale. God is always surprising us with love. Always breaking down our stereotypes, including stereotypes of God. Probably no parable of Jesus does this more effectively than the Prodigal Son. It is a tale of sin, conversion, forgiveness. A tale of leaving home and coming back, a tale of not being condemned but rather of being lavished with love and affection.

Preparation

This prayer assembly is designed as a reconciliation celebration. With some adjustments, an opportunity for private confession and sacramental absolution would be proper. The teens are led through critical transitions of sin and conversion that are evident in the parable. They are given opportunity to reflect in small groups and privately at each of these transitions.

Time to Listen

Leader (setting the context): Jesus wanted us to get the true picture of how God feels about us, even though we don't always feel we deserve much love. So, he did what he did best: he told a parable.

Jesus: There was a man who had two sons. The younger of them said to his father:

Younger Son: Father, give me the share of the property that will be mine.

Jesus: The son gathered all he had and traveled to a distant country, and there he squandered his property in dissolute living.

Response—First Transition

Invite the teens to discuss some examples of how sin is some form of choosing one's own direction, one's own way of living, even though another may seem wiser. Sin is leaving some kind of bond or commitment. In summary, it is a choice to live according to one's own dictates. After a brief discussion, ask the teens to reflect in silence on the most serious example in their own lives of this kind of choice.

Time to Listen

Leader (setting the context): When we make bad choices, choosing our own selfish way, living according to our own dictates, we soon have an opportunity to "wise up." Bad choices can have a built-in warning...even a built-in punishment. Jesus continues with his story:

Jesus: When the younger son had spent everything, a severe famine took place throughout that country, and he began to be in need. So he went and hired himself out to one of the citizens of that country, who sent him to his fields to feed the pigs. He would gladly have filled himself with the pods that the pigs were eating; and no one gave him anything.

Response—Second Transition

Invite the teens to share some examples of a built-in warning and even punishment that is associated with bad choices. What kind of results do our selfish choices engender?

After a period of sharing, challenge the teens to reflect privately on how this has played out in their own choices, especially recently. What is going on now in their lives that is a warning of this kind?

Time to Listen

Leader (setting the context): When it finally hits home that we have made some bad choices, we have the opportunity to change things, to return to a better way of living. Jesus continues with his story.

Jesus: When the younger son came to himself, he said:

Younger Son: How many of my father's hired hands have enough bread and even some to spare, but here I am dying of hunger! I will get up and go to my father, and I will say to him, "Father, I have sinned against heaven and before you; I am no longer worthy to be called your son; treat me like one of your hired hands."

Jesus: So he set off and went to his father.

Response—Third Transition

Invite the teens to discuss what influences them to make important changes. Urge them to be very realistic and honest about this. What are some common steps that they take? What are their feelings at that time? How do they feel about facing a person they have hurt in the past? Do *they* ever rehearse their "return" to the good graces of the person they hurt? After sharing in their small group, give them the opportunity for private reflection about their current need to "return" to some relationship ... to God.

Time to Listen

Leader (setting the context): At this point Jesus' parable turns ordinary thinking upside down and inside out. Ordinarily we expect a hurt person to demand some kind of apology, punishment, or repentance. And traditionally we have expected the God of justice to do the same. But...

Jesus: So the younger son set off and went to his father. But while he was still far off, his father saw him and was filled with compassion; he ran and put his arms around him and kissed him. Then the son said to him:

Younger Son: Father, I have sinned against heaven and before you; I am no longer worthy to be called your son.

Jesus: But the father said to his slaves:

Father: Quickly, bring out a robe—the best one—and put it on him; put a ring on his finger and sandals on his feet. And get the fatted calf and kill it, and let us eat and celebrate; for this son of mine was dead and is alive again; he was lost and is found!

Jesus: And they began to celebrate.

Response—Fourth Transition

Ask the teens to share in small groups some of their experiences of "coming home," renewing friendships, apologizing for causing some kind of hurt. What was the response of the person who was hurt? Have the teens ever experienced someone saying "That's okay ... just forget about it ... I forgive you...." How did they feel?

Invite the teens to spend some time in reflection, thinking about someone they would like to "welcome back home." Then encourage a symbolic ritual. Ask each one to pick someone *to stand in for a real person they have hurt* or have left in some way, and to say to that person: "I need to feel welcomed back, forgiven, loved...." Encourage signs of reconciliation at this time: hugs, handshakes, etc. The teens may want to ask more than one person to show this welcome and forgiveness.

Response—Final Transition

Leader: No one feels better about your "coming home" again than God. No matter how far we go, how wrong our choices, how great the hurt we cause, God our Father is waiting with arms wide open to welcome us back. There is no punishment, no "I told you so's." Just "Let's celebrate!"

Assembly Prayer

(Note: This would be a good time for private confession and absolution if a sacramental minister is available. If not, have someone represent God and church to show each teen some clear sign of love, forgiveness, reconciliation. With music playing, each teen approaches the representative who lays hands on each one's head or shoulder for a moment, and then gives a sincere hug.)

Of Related Interest...

Seasonal Prayer Services for Teenagers
Greg Dues

16 prayer services that help teenagers understand the
themes found in the holidays of the seasons, the church
year and the civic year.
ISBN: 0-89622-473-2, 70 pp, $9.95

Teen Prayer Services
20 Themes for Reflection
Kevin Regan

Helps teens touch life by inviting them into dialogue
with God. Services focus on issues important to teens.
Great for retreats, special sessions and regular classes.
ISBN: 0-89622-520-8, 80 pp, $9.95

Faith Alive
A New Presentation of Catholic Belief and Practice
edited by Rowanne Pasco & John Redford

A panoramic view of the Catholic church, its teachings,
history and traditions. A contemporary, in-depth
portrait excellent for teenagers and young adults.
ISBN: 0-89622-408-2, 320 pp, $9.95

Quicksilvers
Ministering with Junior High Youth
Carole Goodwin

Deals with the unique developmental characteristics,
personal needs, crisis issues and faith concerns of
young adolescents.
ISBN: 0-89622-519-4, 96 pp, $7.95

*Available at religious
bookstores or from*

**TWENTY-THIRD
PUBLICATIONS**
P.O. Box 180
Mystic, CT 06355
1-800-321-0411